Cambridge El<

C000256423

Elements in the Philosophy
edited by
Penelope Rush
University of Tasmania

PLATO WAS *NOT* A MATHEMATICAL PLATONIST

Elaine Landry
University of California, Davis'

CAMBRIDGE
UNIVERSITY PRESS

Shaftesbury Road, Cambridge CB2 8EA, United Kingdom

One Liberty Plaza, 20th Floor, New York, NY 10006, USA

477 Williamstown Road, Port Melbourne, VIC 3207, Australia

314–321, 3rd Floor, Plot 3, Splendor Forum, Jasola District Centre,
New Delhi – 110025, India

103 Penang Road, #05–06/07, Visioncrest Commercial, Singapore 238467

Cambridge University Press is part of Cambridge University Press & Assessment,
a department of the University of Cambridge.

We share the University's mission to contribute to society through the pursuit of
education, learning and research at the highest international levels of excellence.

www.cambridge.org
Information on this title: www.cambridge.org/9781009313780

DOI: 10.1017/9781009313797

When citing this work, please include a reference to the DOI 10.1017/9781009313797

First published 2023

A catalogue record for this publication is available from the British Library.

ISBN 978-1-009-31378-0 Paperback
ISSN 2514-3808 (online)
ISSN 2399-2883 (print)

Plato Was *Not* a Mathematical Platonist

Philosophy of Mathematics

DOI: 10.1017/9781009313797
First published online: January 2023

Elaine Landry
University of California, Davis'

Author for correspondence: Elaine Landry, emlandry@ucdavis.edu

Abstract: This Element argues that Plato was *not* a mathematical Platonist. It shows that Plato keeps a clear distinction between mathematical and metaphysical realism, and the knife he uses to slice the difference is method. The philosopher's dialectical method requires that we tether the truth of hypotheses to existing metaphysical objects. The mathematician's hypothetical method, by contrast, takes hypotheses *as if* they were first principles, so no metaphysical account of their truth is needed. Thus, we come to Plato's methodological as-if realism: In mathematics, we treat our hypotheses *as if* they were first principles, and, consequently, our objects *as if* they existed, and we do this for the purpose of solving problems. Taking the road suggested by Plato's *Republic*, the author shows that some methodological commitments to mathematical objects are made in light of mathematical practice; some are made in light of foundational considerations; and some are made in light of mathematical applicability.

Keywords: Plato, ancient philosophy of mathematics, mathematical realism, mathematical platonism, as-ifism

ISBNs: 9781009313780 (PB), 9781009313797 (OC)
ISSNs: 2514-3808 (online), 2399-2883 (print)

Contents

Indeed, this is why, at the end of Book 7, Plato likens the faculty of thought to that of imagination and, as a consequence, comes to reserve the term "knowledge" for philosophical knowledge *only*. Thus, taking my evidence primarily from the Divided Line analogy and Book 7, I will argue that Plato was not a mathematical Platonist; mathematical objects are not forms, they do not either exist in some metaphysical realm or fix the truth of mathematical statements, and we do not come to know them via recollection.

2 The Interpretive Lay of the Land

The number of interpretations of Plato's views of mathematics is vast. Some consider the whole of Plato's works, others focus on specific dialogues. My interpretation will focus primarily on what Plato says in the *Republic*'s Divided Line and Book 7. The reason for this is twofold; except for the *Meno*, these are the only places where Plato presents a sustained account of mathematics, and there seems little debate that this dialogue was written by Plato.[7] In a broad stroke, my interpretation is intended to cut a midpoint between the two prevailing and competing views. The first is the view of Cornford (1932), White (1976), Tait (2002), and Benson (2006; 2010; 2012) that the hypothetical method is *part of* the dialectical method so that mathematical objects must, in some sense, be *part of* the realm of forms. The second is the view of Burnyeat (2000) and Broadie (2020) that the mathematician's hypothetical method is *distinct from* the philosopher's dialectical method, but that Plato adopts a quietist stance on the ontological status of mathematical objects – that is, on the question of whether mathematical objects are to be taken as *distinct from* forms.

Benson's *part of* view has a long history and is well captured by Cornford's argument that Plato has two types of dialectic at play, each with its own methodology: one mathematical and having as its objects mathematical forms, the other philosophical, or ethical, and having as its objects forms like Justice, Virtue, and Good. Likewise, Benson (2012) sees both types as part of the same method, but further distinguishes between the mathematician's *dianoetic* method and the philosopher's *dialectic* method, arguing that

> the distinction is less a distinction between two different methods, than one between *two different applications* of the *same method*. Both the dianoetician and the dialectician apply or use the method of hypothesis, but the former does so *inadequately and incorrectly*. The dianoetician [as exemplified by

---

[7] I have analyzed what Plato tells us of the benefits and limits of the mathematician's method in the *Meno* (Landry 2012). While there is a discussion of mathematics in the *Seventh Letter*, it is far from clear whether this work is Plato's.

"current practitioners" of mathematics], unlike the dialectician, ... *mistakes* her hypothesis for *archai* [for unhypothetical first principles].

(pp. 1–2; italics added)

Most *part of* interpreters hold that these unhypothetical first principles are unhypothetical because they are tethered to, or fixed by, a stable *metaphysical* domain (i.e., by a realm of mathematical objects taken as *philosophical* forms, or, like Tait, by a realm of foundational mathematical objects taken as *geometric* forms).

Burnyeat (2000), in contrast, uses his *distinct from* interpretation to point to two stances that one may adopt as regards the ontological status of mathematical objects: the "internal" stance taken by practicing mathematicians and the "external" metaphysical stance taken by the philosopher of mathematics. He remains oddly silent on what the practicing mathematician's internal stance comes to but, as regards the latter, holds that Plato "leaves the external question tantalisingly open" (p. 22). Likewise, Broadie (2020) holds that "Plato shows no interest in this metaphysical question" (p. 15).

Benson (2000) similarly holds that "Plato is less concerned to offer a fourfold ontology associated with the four sections of the Line, than he is to describe the correct method of the greatest *mathēma* – the knowledge of the Form of the Good" (p. 1). But, as we have noted, Benson, as many other interpreters who believe that the philosopher's method *must* be adopted by the mathematician, holds that this external question *must* be answered. The various, what I will call, *metaphysical* interpretations that seek to answer this external question agree that one must adopt a mathematical Platonist position but bifurcate over whether this should be answered at a philosophical or at a metamathematical level – that is, whether one must adopt the view that mathematical objects are philosophical forms themselves or are to be founded on an ontologically preferred metamathematical theory of forms, such as foundational theory of geometric forms.

Another option, however, is to argue that mathematical objects are "intermediates" between philosophical forms and sensible objects. Indeed, forgoing his internal/external distinction for the moment, Burnyeat's (2000) position seems to purposefully leave open the possibility of an interpretation of mathematical objects as intermediates:[8]

---

[8] As too does Broadie: "Plato also postulates two correspondingly different levels of intelligible reality, the forms proper and the distinct 'intermediate' or mathematicals which we know from Aristotle came to be posited in Plato's school" (p. 15). McLarty (2005) also argues for an "intermediates" position: "Glaucon in Plato's *Republic* fails to grasp intermediates. He confused pursuing a goal (of searching for first principles) with achieving it, and so he (mistakenly) adopts 'mathematical platonism'" (p. 115). See also Foley's (2008) article, for an illuminating discussion of how the ratios and the proportions of the line can be used to partition debates about the

> That is the main result of the Divided Line passage (511c–d): the introduction of a new intermediate epistemic state, which turns out to have an intermediate degree of clarity when it is compared, on the one side with the ordinary person's opinion about sensibles, and on the other with the dialectician's understanding of Forms. Socrates can then correlate this intermediate degree of cognitive clarity with the intermediate degree of truth or reality which belongs to the non-sensible objects that mathematicians talk about (511d–e).
>
> (p. 42)

However, even if he leaves himself open to an "intermediates" interpretation, Burnyeat does forestall those aforementioned Platonist interpretations, like Benson's, that require that mathematicians or philosophers of mathematics adopt the dialectical method on the basis of a supposed criticism that the mathematicians problematically mistake their hypotheses for unhypothetical first principles and, in so doing, leave their hypotheses unaccounted for. I agree with Burnyeat, and, as I will show, it is this criticism that itself is *the* mistake of all *part of* interpretations. As Burnyeat rightly notes, 'mathematics is not criticised but *placed*. Its intermediate placing in the larger epistemological and ontological scheme of the *Republic* will enable it to play a pivotal, and highly positive, role in the education of future rulers' (p. 42).

Next we must ask: What is this important role? We are told that an education in mathematics will enable the philosopher to grasp the Good, but how does that work? Why does this education take ten years?[9] What is Plato's criticism of mathematics as currently practiced? Why are the branches of mathematics so ordered? Finally, what is the relationship between mathematical reasoning and philosophical/moral reasoning? With respect to the last question, I begin by noting my agreement with Broadie's (2020) claim that 'the text of the *Republic* offers virtually *no evidence* that his [Plato's] problem lies in meta-mathematical ambition for dialectic or in the theory that ethical reality itself is mathematically structured' (p. 29; italics added).

I fully agree with the first of these disjuncts but disagree somewhat with the second. As regards the first disjunct, when we focus on what the text says, we will see that Plato's problem is set at making space for the beneficial role that mathematics plays in preparing the mind for philosophical dialectic, by turning us away from a reliance on beliefs and opinions founded on sense experience. He is also showing us the limits of mathematical inquiry, namely, that it is

---

ontological status of mathematical objects, and his critical analysis of how these considerations impact upon the various "intermediates" interpretations.

[9] We are told in the *Republic* (537b–e) that our philosopher in training is to spend ten years, between the ages of twenty and thirty, studying the mathematical subjects that, as children, "they learned in no particular order," now aiming to "bring [them] together into a unified vision of their kinship with one another and with the nature of what is."

conjectural and so cannot yield the kind of fixity demanded of philosophical knowledge.[10]

This conjectural aspect of mathematics, against all *part of* interpretations, is no criticism of its current practitioners – that is, it is no problem of the method of mathematics that needs fixing by some metaphysical or metamathematical account of its hypothesis as unhypothetical first principles. Again, as Broadie notes:

> [T]he claim [of the superiority of dialectic over mathematics] is not based on any intrinsic contempt on Plato's part for mathematics, for he is going to make mathematics, in its fullest development across all its known branches, the basis of future rulers' training in dialectic ... Yet emphasizing the greatness of mathematics only serves to bring out the surpassing importance of dialectic. (p. 19)

What I will show is that, to appreciate both the benefits and the limits of the method of mathematics and measure these against benefits of the method of philosophy, these methods must be kept distinct, and, consequently, so too must both their epistemology and their ontology.

So, against all of Cornford, White, Tait, Benson, Burnyeat, and Broadie, I will show that Plato *is* concerned to offer a fourfold ontology associated with the four sections of the Divided Line. As I will argue, only then can we understand why mathematical inquiry, while distinct from philosophical inquiry, is "good for the soul." Thus, it is a mistake to claim, as Broadie does, that Plato, in so separating the method of mathematics from that of philosophy, "went well beyond what was needed for making it clear that philosophical thinking, in particular the sort of ethical thinking that would be engaged in by philosophers-rules like those of Plato's ideal state, is not mathematical in character and is not to be modelled on mathematics" (p. 22).

With Burnyeat,[11] I will disagree with Broadie; there is certainly textual evidence for the claim that philosophical or moral reasoning *is* to be modeled on mathematics. By placing the mathematical theory of proportion as the

---

[10] As Broadie notes, "the cognitive superiority – of dialectic to mathematics – in fact the *huge* cognitive superiority of dialectic to mathematics – is the main thing that Plato wants to convey by means of the image of the Divided Line" (p. 13). I am not convinced, however, that it's the *main thing* that Plato wants to convey; on my interpretation, Plato wants to convey, in the Divided Line and in Book 7, both the benefits and the limits of the method of mathematics. I have gone into more detail on the benefits and limits of the method of mathematics in the *Meno* elsewhere (Landry 2012).

[11] See Burnyeat's (2000) claim: "The mathematics and meta-mathematics prescribed for further rulers is much more that instrumental training for the mind. They are somehow supposed to bring an enlargement of ethical understanding" (p. 46). I disagree with him, however, that "*dialectical* debate about the conceptual foundations of mathematics is itself, as a very abstract level, a debate about values like justice" (p. 46; italics added). Here, I will agree with Broadie that making the

highest theory and the Good as the *highest form*, Plato is showing us that even though their methods are distinct, moral reasoning is to be taken as "akin to" mathematical reasoning.

Indeed, I will argue that not only does this supposition answer why the mathematical branches are so ordered, again with the metamathematical theory of proportion itself as the highest theory, but it also answers *the* question of why the study of mathematics is good for the soul, namely, because the "concord" and "harmony," or the *good order*, of both the objects of the branches of mathematics and the objects of philosophy are to be accounted for by proportional reasoning. So, while the ethical realm is not structured by mathematics per se, the proportional structure of the realm of forms is to be taken as "akin to" the proportional structure of the realm of mathematical objects in the sense that the good order of the forms themselves is to be accounted for by the mathematical notion of proportion. Thus, Plato's criticism of mathematics as currently practiced is not, as *part of* interpretations build their case on, that it makes use of hypotheses. Rather, it is that its arguments are taken to rely on sense experience (e.g., "counted units" in the case of arithmetic, "constructed diagrams and figures" in the case of theories of geometry, "ornaments of the heavens" in the case of theories of astronomy, and "audible concordances" in the case of · theories of cosmology).

In our investigation into the order of the branches of mathematics, what we will further see, however, is that the geometrical theory of proportion plays a double role: as Plato's preferred mathematical theory of cosmology and as the highest, or metamathematical, theory that provides a *good ordering* of the branches of mathematics. In this metamathematical use, the mathematician qua philosopher-in-training will come to see that the notion of proportion itself is to be taken as a measure of harmony and concord itself. It is this use, when next applied to the philosopher's forms, that will lend itself to the philosopher's inquiry into moral matters and, in so doing, get them closer to grasping the Good as the highest form – that is, it will allow the philosopher to see, via the use of proportional reasoning, the sense in which the Good itself provides a *good ordering* of the forms.

Finally, I will appeal to this account of the metamathematical use of a geometric theory of proportion to conclude that Plato does take a stand on the "external" question, answering clearly that mathematical objects are not forms, either philosophical or foundational. Keeping in mind what Plato shows by placing mathematical objects within the realm of Being, and what the *Republic*

---

metamathematical debate a *dialectical* debate will lead to "the obverse idiocy of demanding that mathematics should model itself on ethical philosophizing" (p. 23).

says – namely, that "philosophic natures always love the sort of learning that makes clear to them *some feature of being that always is* and does not wander around between coming to be and decaying" (485b; italics added) – we will see that mathematical objects must have some "feature of being" but, again, only hypothetically so. Thus, and against both quietest and Platonist interpretations, I will argue that, as regards mathematical objects, Plato is a methodological realist – that is, he is a realist on the basis of what objects of thought are needed to solve both mathematical and metamathematical problems.

More pointedly, as regards the latter problems, what the geometrical theory of proportion brings to the mathematician's table is an answer to the *internal* metamathematical question: What branch of mathematics *accounts for* or *good orders* the other branches of mathematics? What the geometric theory of proportion brings to both the mathematician's and the philosopher's table is talk of harmony and concord itself (i.e., talk of *good order* itself, as expressed by reasoning in terms of proportions). Indeed, as we will see, this is why the Divided Line is so divided into the geometric ratios that it is! I will show that the use of proportional reasoning itself plays an overarching and essential role in three ways: (a) in the overall argument scheme of the Divided Line and in Book 7, the notion of clarity, as a measure of truth and reality, is accounted for by the proportion of ratios between the lines themselves;[12] (b) in his account of the good order of the branches of mathematics; and (c) in his account of the good order of the forms. This last explains why the study of mathematics is needed to grasp the Good.

So, against the *quietist* interpretations of Burnyeat and Broadie, Plato does answer the "external" questions of the ontological status of mathematical objects and the metamathematical sense in which mathematical objects are "akin." However, against the *part of* interpretations of Cornford, White, Benson, and Tait, he does this by reducing both questions to *internal* questions – that is, to problems that themselves can be answered via the mathematician's hypothetical method. Simply, then, the philosopher's dialectical method and its need to appeal to an external philosophical or foundational realm is made mute. Plato's mathematician is a methodological realist, they are *not* a metaphysical realist; they take mathematical hypothesis *as if* they were true first principles for the purpose of solving a problem and, in virtue of this, they take mathematical objects *as if* they exist. Thus, to require of mathematics that its objects are forms, be these philosophical or foundational forms, is to mistakenly confuse both the method and the epistemology of mathematics with that of philosophy. Finally, and now in hand with Plato, my counsel, as regards current practitioners of philosophy of mathematics, is as follows: We too would do well to keep the

---

[12] Smith (2018) provides a more detailed analysis of Plato's use of the notion of clarity.

methodological requirements for mathematics distinct from those of philosophy – that is, we would do well to place more focus on the mathematician's method and so on mathematical practice than we do on philosophical metaphysics or mathematical foundations.

3 The Divided Line

In Book 6 of the *Republic*, in attempting to explain the nature of the Good itself, Socrates first uses the Sun analogy to show the way in which the Sun is an "offspring" (506e) of the Good, and thereby comes to separate the visible and the intelligible realms. Next, Socrates uses the Divided Line analogy to further explain the epistemic and ontic distinctions that result from the distinctions between the visible and intelligible. Following Glaucon's claim that he has, through Socrates' use of the Sun analogy, understood "these two kinds" (the visible and the intelligible) (509d), Socrates introduces the Divided Line analogy to further explain his claim that "what the latter (the Good) is in the intelligible realm in relation to understanding and intelligible things, the former (the Sun) is in the visible realm in relation to sight and visible things" (508c). Bringing the two analogies together, Socrates begins with the assumption that the Sun is "sovereign" over the visible realm and the Good is "sovereign" over the intelligible realm (509e).

Socrates then subdivides each realm, according to the *clarity* of its objects:

> Represent them, then, by a line *divided into two unequal sections*. Then divide each section – that of the visible and that of the intelligible – *in the same ratio* as the line. In terms now of *relative clarity and opacity*, you will have as one subsection of the visible, *images*. By images I mean, first, shadows, then reflections in bodies of water and in all close-packed, smooth, and shiny materials, and everything of that sort. Do you understand? (509d–510a; italics added)

It is important to pause here to note that the notion of clarity and the *ratios* of clarity as set by the various divisions and subdivisions are here intended to do both epistemic and ontological work. As Plato himself remarks,

> when it [the soul] focuses on something that is *illuminated both* by *truth and what is*, it *understands*, *knows*, and manifestly possesses understanding. But when it focuses on what is mixed with obscurity, on what comes to be and passes away, it *believes* and is dimmed ... and seems *bereft of understanding*.
> (508d; italics added)

Given Glaucon's assent that he has understood both the distinction between the intelligible and the visible realm and the nature of the objects of the first, opaque, subsection of the visible realm, Socrates next considers the objects of the clear subsection, and moves to consider the ontic and epistemic consequences of these distinctions made within this realm:

> [I]n the other subsection of the visible, put the *originals of these images* – that is, the animals around us, every plant, and the whole class of manufactured things ... . Would you be willing to say, then, that, *as regards truth and untruth,* the *division is in this ratio:* as what is *believed* is to what is *known*, so *the likeness is to the thing it is like*? (510a; italics added)

Thus, physical objects themselves and their images respectively relate, on the basis of the ratio of their clarity or opacity (which is illuminated by the Sun [508b]), *ontologically* to existence and nonexistence, and *epistemically* to truth and untruth, and so to knowledge and opinion.

We subsequently come to the subdivisions of the intelligible realm:

> Next, consider how the section of the intelligible is to be divided ... As follows: in one subsection, the soul *using as images the things that were imitated before,* is *forced to* base its inquiry on *hypothesis*, proceeding not to a first principle, but to a conclusion. In the other subsection, *by contrast*, it makes its way to an *unhypothetical first principle*, proceeding from a hypothesis, but without the images used in the previous subsection, using *forms themselves* and making its investigation through them. (510b)

In the first subsection of the intelligible realm, then, the soul uses "images"[13] and its method is such that it is *forced to*[14] base its inquiry on hypotheses, reasoning from a hypothesis down to a conclusion.

In the other subsection, the soul reasons from a hypothesis up to an unhypothetical first principle and then down to a conclusion,[15] making no use of images but only of forms themselves. Glaucon is here confused, and so Socrates begins anew, now making mention of the mathematicians' method:

> Let's try again. You see, you will understand it more easily after the explanation. I think you know that students of geometry, calculation, and the like *hypothesize the odd* and *the even, the various figures, the three kinds of angles*, and other things akin to these in each of their investigations,

---

[13] As we will see, it is best to think of a diagram or figure as an example of what is meant here by "image."

[14] What explains the *fundamental* difference between my interpretation and Benson's (and many others; see, for example, works by Tait [2002], Robinson [1953], and Annas [1981]) is that I, like Burnyeat (2000), do not take the fact that mathematicians are "forced to" use hypotheses as the criticism made by Plato of current practitioners and then use this to argue that the mathematician, like the philosopher, must take up the dialectical method. Here I agree with Burnyeat (and McLarty [2005]) that hypotheses are taken by Plato as "intrinsic to the nature of mathematical thought ... To demand that the mathematicians give an account of their initial hypotheses ... would be to make them stop doing mathematics and do something else instead ... . It is thus no criticism to say that mathematicians give no account of their hypotheses. It is simply to say that mathematics is what they are doing, not dialectic" (pp. 37–38).

[15] This is yet another reason why, against Cornford, White, and Benson's view, the hypothetical method cannot be taken as *part of* the dialectical method; for the first method, the soul reasons *down* from a hypothesis, for the second it reasons *up* from a hypothesis to an unhypothetical first principle.

regarding them as known. These they treat as absolute hypotheses and *do not think it necessary to give any argument for them,* either to themselves or to others, *as if* they were *evident to everyone.* And going from these first principles through the remaining steps, they arrive in full agreement at *the point they set out to reach in their investigation.* (510c–d; italics added)

Note, then, that the objects of mathematics are *not* the previously mentioned "images," but they are "the odd," "the even," "the various figures," and so on. These objects are treated *both* as hypothesized *and* as known, so no account of them is needed. They are taken *as if* they were "evident to everyone" first principles, but they are not. Indeed, as noted in the last sentence, the purpose of the mathematicians' *as if* hypotheses are to solve a given problem, so, unlike the philosophers' method, the mathematicians' method is not aimed at arriving at *un*hypothetical first principles, it is aimed at solving problems. This is another reason why the hypothetical method cannot be *part of* the dialectical method; mathematical hypotheses are taken *as known* – that is, *as if* they were first principles, so no account of them is needed – whereas philosophical hypotheses are taken as hypotheses, so, if they are to be held as known, *an account* of them in terms of unhypothetical first principles is needed.[16]

Having so clarified things to Glaucon's satisfaction, Socrates is now ready to move on:

Then don't you also know that they *use* visible forms and make their arguments about them [talk about them[17]], although they are *not thinking about them,* but about those other *things that they are like.* They *make their arguments* with a view to *the square itself* and *the diagonal itself, not the diagonal they draw* and similarly with the others. The very things they make and draw, of which shadows and reflections in water are images, they now in turn *use as images* in seeking to see *those other things themselves* that one cannot see except by means of *thought.* (510d–511a; italics added)

There is a much missed and important distinction to be made here between "images," or what a mathematician *uses* or *talks about* (e.g., the diagonal they draw) and "things themselves," or what they *think about* (e.g., the diagonal itself).[18] Drawn diagrams, figures, and so on are "only images" used to *aid* the

---

[16] Cherniss (1951) holds a similar view.

[17] Here I prefer Shorey's (1994) translation as "talk about them" because, as we will see, I do not think Plato would allow for making arguments about images.

[18] Indeed, in most mathematical Platonist interpretations of this passage, the use of term "itself" is standardly appealed to argue that the distinction here is between mathematical "images" and mathematical objects "themselves" as forms. But as Burnyeat rightly points out,

The issue is whether that little word "itself" signals reference to a Platonic Form, as in phrases like "justice itself" (517e1–2) ... The word "itself" is certainly not decisive on its own, otherwise a Form of thirst would intrude (437e4) into Book IV's analysis of the

mathematician's thinking about the "things themselves"; their arguments, how-ever, are intended to be about the objects they think about. There is also a much missed and important, but often confused, analogy that Plato will appeal to further on: that just as physical objects are the originals of "shadowy" physical images, so mathematical objects are the originals of "shadowy" mathematical images; just as for the objects of the physical realm wherein "the likeness [the image] is to the thing it is like [the original]," so too for the objects of the mathematical realm. As originals, then, mathematical objects are clearer, and recalling the epistemic and ontic role of the concept of clarity as a marker of truth and existence, statements about them are truer and they are more real than those about mathematical "images." Thus, when the mathematician uses the faculty of *thought* they will come to use diagrams and figures "as only images," and, as a result, will come to see the need to make their arguments about mathematical objects themselves.[19] However, these mathematical "kinds of things" (i.e., kinds that arise out of the use of the hypothetical method), while both intelligible and clearer than their "images," are yet distinct from those that arise out of the use of the dialectical method:

> This, then, is the *kind of thing* that I said was intelligible. The soul is *forced to use* hypotheses in the investigations of it, not traveling up to a first principle, since *it cannot escape or get above its hypotheses*, by using as images those very things of which images were made by the things below them, and which, by comparison to their images, were thought to be clear and to be honored as such. (511a; italics added)

The mathematician, then, has access to objects that are found in the intelligible realm, but that are distinct from the other intelligible kinds of things (forms), both *methodologically* because is the mathematician is forced to use hypotheses and *ontologically* because the objects are objects of thought. So, again using the

---

divided soul ... "the diagonal itself" is opposed to "the diagonal *they draw*" ... the context *is mathematics, not metaphysics*. It is to mathematics, then, that we should look to judge the effect of the word "itself." (pp. 35–37; italics added)

I agree, but, as I will show, while the context here is mathematics, the proportional reasoning afforded by the Divided Line, does carry with it ontological weight. So, one *cannot* conclude, as Burnyeat (2000) does, that "Socrates is reporting what practicing mathematicians do and say, not offering his own philosophical account of the ontological status of mathematical objects" (p. 33).

[19] So, contrary to some claims, it is not that Plato is critical of mathematicians' *use* of diagrams; he is critical of those who *make their arguments on the basis* of such diagrams (e.g., a diagram of a square). What the mathematician must do is recognize that these are but "images" of the object itself (e.g., images of square itself), only then will they come to realize that they must make their arguments on the basis of the object itself. As we will see, it is this criticism that is consistent with Plato's criticisms, in Book 7, of current practitioners of mathematics: that they make their arguments on the basis of something physical, be these physical images, physical sounds, and so on.

intended proportional reasoning as set out by the ratios of clarity in the divided line, just as the images of physical objects are less clear than physical objects themselves, and mathematical images are less clear than mathematical objects, so too are mathematical objects less clear than the philosophical objects grasped by traveling up to a first principle: the forms. That Plato intends to use these methodological differences to further infer even more epistemic *and* ontic distinctions is next made clear:

> Also understand, then, that by the other subsection of the intelligible I mean what *reason* itself grasps by the power of *dialectical discussion*, treating its hypotheses, not as first principles, but as *genuine hypotheses*, in order to arrive at what is *unhypothetical* and *the first principle* of everything. Having grasped this principle, it reverses itself and, keeping hold of what follows from it, comes down to a conclusion, making no use of anything visible at all, but only of *forms themselves*, moving on through forms to forms, and ending in forms.[20] (511b–c; italics added)

Glaucon is here more than confused; indeed, he is both shocked and surprised by the implications of these methodological differences:

> I understand, though not adequately – you see, in my opinion, you are speaking of an enormous task. You want to distinguish the part of what is and what is intelligible, the part looked at by the science of *dialectical discussion, as clearer than the part* [*as something truer and more exact than the objects*] looked at by the so-called sciences – those for which *hypotheses are first principles* [assumptions are *arbitrary starting points*].[21]

---

[20] Benson (2012) takes another passage (511a–c) as but another point where Plato's criticism of current practitioners of mathematics makes it mark – that is, they are "forced to" use hypotheses and do not take them as "genuine," and so do not see that the hypothetical method is only a first step toward the search for unhypothetical first principles. This has the added consequence that until they come to adopt the dialectic method, they, as Burnyeat (2000) suggests for quite different reasons, ought to maintain a quietist stance with respect to ontological matters. As Benson (2012) explains: "Plato is not indicating that the method of mathematics is incapable of pursuing such an ontological inquiry. Rather, the claim is descriptive rather than prescriptive. Mathematics (when it is contrasted with pure dialectic) or, perhaps better, philosophical *dianoetic* pursues its inquiry only so far, recognizes that its procedure is incomplete, and so hands over its results to the pure dialectician" (p. 28). As I will show, however, the mathematician need not make this move to dialectic; the geometric theory of proportion can be used to provide an account of the mathematicians' hypotheses, without having to give their metamathematical account in terms of unhypothetical first principles, and so without having to "hand over the results to the pure dialectician." It is *only* the philosopher, then, who by use of their dialectical method, must treat their hypotheses as "genuine hypotheses" and so who must seek to give an account of them in terms of objects that fix or tether their hypothesis as first principles (i.e., in terms of "forms themselves").

[21] Here I also give Shorey's translation because it better captures the use of the notion of clarity as a measure of truth and existence and the arbitrary, or conjectural, aspect of the mathematician's hypotheses.

And although those who look at the latter part are forced to do so by means of *thought* rather than *sense perception*, still, because they do not go back to a genuine first principle in considering it, but proceed from hypotheses, *you do not think that they have true understanding* of them, even though – given such a first principle – they are intelligible. And you seem to me to call the state of mind of the geometers – and the others of that sort – *thought* but *not understanding*; thought being *intermediate*[22] between <u>belief</u> and understanding. (511c–d; italics added)

Again, using the ratio of clarity as his cleaver, Plato comes to consider the full epistemological *and* ontological implications of these differences in method.[23] That is, epistemic truth and ontic reality is to be given *only* to those intelligibles that are reached by the philosophers' dialectical method. Next employing proportional reasoning as fixed by the ratios of clarity across the realms, we have that the mathematicians' objects are more clear (true/real) than all of physical objects, physical images, and mathematical images because they are

---

[22] I thank an anonymous referee for motivating me to note here the claim "even though – given such a first principle – they are intelligible" and the claim that thought is "intermediate," when combined with the 510d–e talk of "the square itself" and "the diagonal itself" gives rise to another route to a Platonist interpretation. On this interpretation, Plato is here presenting the mathematicians' hypothetical method and the philosophers' dialectical method as different ways of investigating the same kind of intelligible objects: forms, resulting in two different epistemic states – thought of forms and understanding of forms. This Platonist reading is intended as being analogous to the way in which one may study physical objects in two different ways resulting in two different epistemic states – belief when of the objects themselves or imagination when of an image of a physical object. Such a reading allows, on the one hand, for a full-blown Platonist reading of mathematical objects as forms, and, on the other, by focusing on Plato's use of the term "intermediate" here, for an Aristotelian reading of mathematical objects as an "intermediate" between physical objects and philosophical forms. There are two problems with either interpretation, both already noted by Burnyeat. The first (see n. 13) is the problematic appeal to the use of the term "itself" to imply that reference to a form is intended. The second is that the analogy upon which it rests is mistakenly interpreted. As already noted, the analogy that Plato presents us with is *not* between physical objects and their images and intelligible objects (qua philosophical forms) and their images (qua mathematical forms), rather it is between physical objects and their images and mathematical objects and their images (diagrams or figures). Again, as Burnyeat (p. 36) rightly points out, the analogy is between "the diagonal itself" and "the diagonal *they draw*." However, to fully undermine these lingering Platonist interpretations, we are still left to deal with the status of claim "even though – given such a first principle – they are intelligible," which yet seems to suggest that mathematical objects are forms or, at least, an "intermediate" kind of object known via first principles. I will deal with this concern in detail when we come to investigate what Plato says in Book 7, especially 531d–534c, where the role of first principles is *re*considered on the basis of a new analogy between thought and imagination.

[23] As noted, Burnyeat and I agree on the claim that ontological conclusions about the nature of mathematical objects are intended to be inferred from both methodological and epistemological considerations, but he further holds that these inferences hold only "internally," or only within the context of mathematical practice, with the consequence that Plato "has Socrates decline further clarification of the (external, metaphysical) matter" (pp. 34–35). I will show, however, that there is no need to appeal to an internal/external distinction so that ontological considerations can, and indeed should, be drawn from the internal context of both mathematical *and metamathematical* practice.

grasped more clearly, by *thought* and not by the sense perception, *but* because no first-principled account is given of them they remain less clear (true/real) than those intelligible objects grasped by the *understanding*. The Divided Line ends with Plato clarifying, again by reasoning proportionally from the ratios of clarity, the epistemic terminology that he intends to employ:

> You have grasped my meaning most adequately. Join me, then, in taking these four conditions in the soul as *corresponding to* the four subsections of the line: *understanding* dealing with *the highest, thought* dealing with *the second*: assign *belief* to *the third*, and *imagination* [picture thinking or conjecture][24] to *the last*. Arrange them *in a proportion* and consider that *each shares in clarity to the degree that the subsection it deals with shares in truth* [in the same degree as their objects partake of *truth and reality*]. (511d–e)

Thus, reasoning proportionally by taking the ratio of clarity to be the mark of both epistemic truth and ontic reality, we have that in the visible realm, what we believe is truer than our opinions because physical objects are more real than images, and in the intelligible realm, what we think is truer than what we believe because mathematical objects are more real than mathematical images, and finally, what we understand is truer than what we think because forms are more real than mathematical objects. We have, then, our four epistemological states and their corresponding ontological objects: understanding/forms, thought/ mathematical objects, belief/physical objects, and imagination/images of physical objects.

But is this all the evidence we need to claim that mathematical objects are *not* forms? Perhaps too these mathematical objects, as Aristotle reports of Plato's view (*Metaphysics*, 987b), are yet distinct "intermediates."[25] Or, perhaps, as Cornford, White, Tait, and Benson suggest, the mathematician, in light of Plato's "criticisms," could or should be now motivated to adopt the dialectical method and so search for those unhypothetical, metaphysical, or metamathematical first principles that would allow them to *tether* or *account for* their hypotheses. To speak against these possibilities, and clearly conclude that Plato

---

[24] Again, I include Shorey's more detailed translation. Note too that the term Plato uses here for "imagination" is *eikasai*. This word is Plato's own creation, and some translate it as "imagination," as derived from *eikon* or "imagine," and others as "conjecture," as derived from *eikaz* (*estahi*) or "to guess at." We will see, when we come to our interpretation of Book 7, and especially as we consider what Plato says at 534a, why these mixed meanings are not only intentional but are also a crucial part of our coming to understand the way in which the faculty of thought is akin to the faculty of imagination. I thank an anonymous referee for pushing me to make this point explicit.

[25] See Annas (2003) for an excellent overview of Aristotle's interpretations of the various Platonist accounts of mathematical objects. Of course, by "Platonist," I do not mean views held by Plato himself.

was not a mathematical Platonist, we need to next consider what Plato says in Book 7, where, in detailing both the educational value of mathematics and the problems with mathematics as currently practiced, Socrates, again using proportional reasoning based on the ratios of clarity, *re*considers the distinctions of the Divided Line. It is to these *re*considerations that I now turn.

4 Book 7

Just after Book 6's Divided Line analogy, Plato, in Book 7, introduces the Cave analogy[26] to represent "the effect of [a philosophical] education and the lack of it on our nature" (514a), so that the philosophical journey outside the cave, is to be thought of "as the upward journey of the soul to the intelligible realm" (517b). Interestingly, and telling against any need for an epistemological use of a myth of recollection,[27] we are simply told that this analogy shows that the "power to learn is present in everyone's soul" (518c).[28] Thus, education and learning, "takes for granted that sight [and, by analogy, the capacity of the soul, reason] is there" but it is "not turned in the right way" so that we must "contrive to redirect it appropriately" (518d). The aim of Book 7, then, is to show what subject can be used to "redirect" the soul from its downward journey to its upward one, so that the philosopher may come to "see the Good" (519c).

To this end, Socrates asks: "So what subject is it, Glaucon, that draws the soul from what comes to be to what is?" (521d). Glaucon is next pushed to consider "one of those (subjects) that touches all of them" (522b) – that is arithmetic or "number and calculation" (522c). This subject is claimed as "one of the subjects we were looking for that naturally stimulate the understanding" (522e–523). The problem, however, is that "no one uses it correctly" (523a); for example, they see numbers as "attached to visible or tangible bodies" (525d). In its correct use, this subject must "summon thought" and, in so doing, "wake up the understanding" (514d); for example, numbers must be taken as "accessible only to *thought* and grasped on no other way" (526a; italics added). So, the philosopher-in-training and the mathematician must both move away from *becoming* or what *comes to be* (what is grasped by sense perception) toward *being* or what *is* (what is grasped by reason) – that is, they must aim at "knowledge of what is, not of something that comes to be and passes away" (527b). So, in our newly *re*considered divided line,

---

[26] See Burnyeat (2000, pp. 42–56) for an excellent discussion of the significance and role of the Cave analogy, and, specifically, for his analysis of the role that it plays in our understanding of Plato's development of the divided line in Book 7.

[27] As noted by both Landry (2012) and Burnyeat (2000), the theory of recollection *does not* play any epistemic role here. As Burnyeat succinctly states: "(t)he *Republic* makes do with the more modest thesis, shared with Aristotle, that the soul has the capacity to attain knowledge of the world ... " (p. 72).

[28] See also Shorey's translation as "this indwelling power in the soul."

we have an added ontological aspect to the divided line: the physical realm is taken as the realm of *becoming* and the intelligible as the realm of *being*. But note that, in light of the Divided Line's epistemic distinction between mathematical *thought* and philosophical *understanding*, these mathematical subjects serve only to redirect the soul; by summoning or using thought, it stirs or wakes up the understanding. So here too, mathematical objects are to be taken as objects of thought, not objects of understanding.

Plato next notes the manner in which the layman and the current mathematical practitioner reason incorrectly; they use their senses and rely on images (both images of physical objects and images as diagrams and figures of mathematical objects) whereas they should use thought and rely only on those mathematical objects themselves firmly located in the intellectual realm. On their upward journey, then, the philosopher-in-training must first take up arithmetic,

> ... not as laymen do, but staying with it until they reach the point at which they see the nature of numbers by means of the *understanding* itself; not like tradesmen and retailers ... but ... for ease in *turning the soul* itself around from becoming to truth and being (525c) ... It [arithmetic] gives the soul *a strong lead upward and compels it* to discuss the *numbers themselves*, never permitting anyone to propose for discussion numbers attached to visible or tangible bodies ... (525d; italics added)

Lest one be tempted to make much of the use of 'understanding itself' here, note that immediately after we are reminded that such numbers "are accessible only to *thought* and can be grasped in *no other way*" (526a; italics added), and as such arithmetic "really does seem to be necessary to us, since it apparently *compels* the soul to [move upward and] use *understanding itself* on the *truth itself*" (526a–b; italics added).[29] As with arithmetic, likewise too for our account of the subjects of geometry (526c–e); solid geometry (two-dimensional geometry or "whatever shares in depth"); astronomy (three dimensional or "revolving solids") (528b); and, cosmology (theory of harmony) (530d). That is, for all of the branches of mathematics, we are *not* to seek an account of any of these subjects on the basis of how they are currently practiced. We consider first geometry:

> [T]his science *is itself entirely the opposite* of what is said about it in accounts of its current practitioners (527a) ... [they] *talk of* squaring, applying, adding,

---

[29] Note also that Plato will come to switch around the terms "understanding" and "knowledge," so that the term "knowledge" will be reserved for philosophical understanding only, whereas the term "thought" will be reserved for mathematical understanding, as opposed to the term "mathematical knowledge." So, it seems that Plato is using "understanding" here to prepare us for this shift.

and the like, whereas, in fact, the entire subject is *practiced for the sake of acquiring knowledge* … it is knowledge of *what always is*, not of something that comes to be and passes away … in that case … it can *draw the soul upwards toward* truth and produce philosophical *thought* by directing upward what we now wrongly direct downwards. (527b; italics added)

As for solid geometry, we are somewhat mysteriously told

that subject has not even been investigated yet … there are two reasons for that. Because no city values it, it is not vigorously investigated, due to its difficulty. And investigators need a director if they are to discover anything. Now, in the first place, such a director is difficult to find. Second, even if he could be found, *as things stand* now *those who investigate it are too arrogant to obey him* … But if an entire city served as his co-director and took his lead in valuing this subject, then they [these *specialists*] would obey him, and with *consistent and vigorous investigation* would reveal the facts about it [bring out the truth]. For even now, when it is not valued by the masses and *hampered* by investigators who lack any *account of its usefulness* [the *ignorance of their students as to the true reasons for pursuing them*] – all the same, in spite of these handicaps, the force of its appeal [force by way of their *inherent charm*] has caused it to be developed. So, it would not be surprising if the facts about it [truth about them][30] were revealed in any case. (528c)

I believe that Plato is here referring to Theaetetus as his preferred "director"; Theaetetus was both a native of Athens and was known to be developing a theory of solid geometry around the time of the writing of the *Republic*.[31] As I will show, much is at stake here and there are many suggestions as to just who Plato is referring to when he speaks of "those who investigate it who are too arrogant to obey him" and "investigators who lack any account of their usefulness." My claim is that both here, and next when he comes to speak of astronomy as it is "handled today" (529a), he is referring to Archytas and his Pythagorean followers. Not only was Archytas a well-known political figure, so talk of directing a city seems apt, but he was also developing a theory of astronomy (or mechanics more generally) based on a Pythagorean or arithmetical theory of proportion, or a theory of proportion build up out of arithmetic ratios. And, more problematically as a Pythagorean, these ratios for the study of astronomy were taken as arising from sense perception (i.e., what was seen "in the ornaments of the heavens" [529b]), and, for theories of harmonics, they

---

[30]   Again, I include Shorey's more detailed translation.

[31]   As Burnyeat (2000, p. 1) notes: "Plato has Socrates make plans for it (solid geometry) to develop more energetically in the future, because it only came into existence (thanks especially to Theaetetus) well after the dramatic date of the discussion in the *Republic*." I question the claim that this development was "well after" the *Republic*; indeed, I will argue, by appealing to what Plato says in the *Theaetetus*, that Plato was well-aware of Theaetetus' mathematical developments.

were taken as arising from what was heard in "audible concordances" (530c). As Plato sees it, the problem here is twofold: it is both that current practitioners of these mathematical theories rely on sense perception and that they "lacked *an account* of its usefulness."

More to the point, what I will show is that these Pythagoreans lacked a geometrical theory of proportion[32] that could not only provide a mathematical account of both astronomy and cosmology, but that could further provide a metamathematical account of what all mathematical subjects have in common; that is, an account of numbers, figures, motion, and sound in terms of geometric measures or ratios. This claim marks a major point of disagreement with Burnyeat (2000), who assumes that Plato's theory of proportion is, or is to be based on, Archytas' arithmetical theory. Indeed, as we will see, this point of departure provides the basis for several other significant differences between us. My appeal to the use of a geometrical theory of proportion also marks an important point of divergence from all *part of* interpretations, including Tait's (2002). That is, what *part of* interpretations get right is that, for Plato, mathematics itself must be metamathematically "accounted for"; what they get wrong is the demand that such accounts can only be provided by the mathematician taking up the philosopher's dialectical method, which would require reference to a fixed domain of mathematical objects as forms, be these metaphysical forms or foundational geometric forms. Thus, while Tait rightly notes that Plato was "concerned with foundations because of 'the discovery of incommensurable line segments'" (pp. 19–20), I think he, like Burnyeat, is mistaken in his claim that "a geometric theory of proportion has likely still not been discovered by the time of the *Republic*" (p. 20). It might not have been *fully* developed, but Plato's reference, in the *Theaetetus*, to the mathematical work of both Theodorus and Theaetetus shows that he is aware that it is *being developed*.[33]

In line with Benson,[34] I take Archytas, Philolaus and other Pythagoreans as the referents of those current practitioners who both "rely on images" and "fail to give an account," and too I take Theodorus and Theaetetus as the "credible mathematicians." However, I part ways with Benson when he claims that "we would do well to avoid drawing any conclusions concerning the relative flaws and merits of Theodorus' and Theaetetus' procedures" (p. 18). Indeed, as I will argue, it is precisely to their, albeit developing, geometric theory of proportion,

---

[32] See Fowler (2003) for an overview the differences between arithmetic and geometric theories of proportion, and for an insightful, well-researched, and convincing argument that Plato's preference was for a geometric theory.

[33] Note too that Plato and Theaetetus were both students of the Theodorus, who again was known to be working on a geometric theory of proportion, so again it was likely known by Plato at the time of the writing of the *Republic*.

[34] See especially Benson (2012, pp. 16–24).

developed as it was out of the desire to solve mathematical, physical, and metamathematical problems via the use of the mathematician's hypothetical method that we should look to "ascend to problems" (531c) and give "and account of its usefulness" by showing that, metamathematically, it provides an overarching good-ordered account of mathematics itself. Thus, I will argue against all *part of* interpretations by showing that Plato has a different, *organizational* conception of what he intends for a metamathematical foundation.

Having stated and situated my claim and aims, let us now continue onward with what Plato says. We come next to the fourth subject, astronomy "which deals the motion of <u>things having depth</u> [the motion of solids]":

> As it is handled today by those who teach philosophy[35] [are trying to lead us up to philosophy], *it makes the soul look very much downward* ... I mean if someone were looking at something by leaning his head back and studying ornaments on a ceiling ... I would say he never really learns – since there is *no knowledge* to be had of such things – and that his soul is not looking up but down, whether he does his leaning lying on his back on land or on sea! ... But these [the motions of the ornaments] fall far short of the *true* ones – those motions in which things that *are really fast or really slow*, as measured in *true numbers* and as forming all the *true geometrical* figures ... And these, of course, must be grasped by *reason and thought*, not by sight ... Therefore, we should use the ornaments in the heavens *as models* to help us *study these other things*. (529a–e; italics added)

How then shall we be motivated to proceed in our study of astronomy if not by physical images? Simply, we are to use these physical images as physical diagrams and then use these physical diagrams as images of mathematical objects themselves, this with the aim of solving a physical problem by making it a mathematical one; for instance, by measuring the true speed of motions by true numbers as measured between true geometrical figures.

> Just as in geometry, then, it is by *making use of problems*, that we will pursue astronomy too. We will leave the things in the heavens alone if we are really going to participate in astronomy and make the naturally wise element in the soul *useful instead of useless*. (530b; italics added)

So, it is by "making use of problems" and, in so doing, attending to the *usefulness* of our mathematical hypotheses, taken *as if* they are true first principles, that we are led to those true objects that are needed to solve these physical problems, that we are to undertake our study of astronomy. Turing then to the more general account of the usefulness of mathematics, this schema sums

---

[35] Again, I prefer Shorey's translation here. Also, and speaking to my interpretative preference of Theaetetus over Archytas, note here that only Archytas and the Pythagoreans were known as both mathematicians *and* philosophers; Theaetetus was known as a mathematician only.

what I call Plato's *methodological as-ifism*: we take a mathematical object *as if* it exists because we take a hypothesis *as if* it were a true first principle, and we do this with the aim of solving a problem.

Having set our problem-solving strategy, we come next to the fifth and final mathematical subject – that is, the study of the theory of harmony itself. We are first told, as with "astronomical motions" so with "harmonic ones" (530d) – that is, current practitioners, including Pythagoreans[36] (530d) believe that

> it is in these audible concordances that they search for numbers but they do not *ascend to problems* or investigate *which numbers are in* concord and which are not, and *what the explanation is* in each case" (531c; italics added)

It is interesting that Plato uses the term "ascend" here; recall that, on my reading, the mathematician, who adopts the hypothetical method, must travel *down* from hypotheses. So, one might be tempted, as are Cornford, Tait, and Benson (see, for example, Benson [2012, pp. 18–23]), to appeal to this use of 'ascend' to argue that the *only* way the mathematician can ascend is by traveling *up* from hypotheses toward first principles, so that Plato here intends the directive that the mathematician must adopt the dialectical method. My counter point, which I will argue for in the next section, is that Plato, by using the phrase "ascend to *problems*" is here indicating that he intends the albeit emerging geometric theory of proportion as itself, allowing us to "ascend" to those metamathematical problems that concern questions of the "kinds of things" of mathematics and the "kinships" among them, and it does this by providing an overarching account of the lower-level mathematical branches.

Returning to Plato, we note that Glaucon here responds that this "ascending to problems" is a "daimonic task"[37] and Socrates is quick to remind him that it is just this task that is "useful in the search for the beautiful and the good" (531c). As we will see, the mathematician's metamathematical use of the geometric theory of proportion is useful for their overall aim of providing an overarching good-ordering account of the subjects of mathematics itself, and it is just this use that "contributes something" to the philosopher's goal of searching for the good.

> Moreover, I take it that if the *investigation of all the subjects* we have mentioned arrives at *what they share in common* with one another and what

---

[36] Again, given that Plato explicitly mentions Pythagoreans here, and given that Archytas was both a well-known politician and Pythagorean astronomer, this speaks strongly to my claim that Plato does *not* see Archytas' arithmetical theory of proportion as useful for any of the study of either geometric solids, astronomy, or harmony.

[37] Note here the double meaning of the Greek term *diamon*; meaning both god-like and to divide. So, the metamathematician's god-like task is to divide the mathematical branches in a way that further good orders them.

> their affinities are, and *draws conclusions about their kinship*, it does con-
> tribute *something to our goal* and is not labor in vain; *but otherwise, it is in*
> *vain* (531d; italics added)

So, in addition to its being among the five mathematical subjects, the *math-*
ematical value and *philosophical use* of the geometric theory of proportion is
that it allows us to give a good-ordering account of what all the other mathematical subjects have in common, and, in so doing, it is the highest subject that
allows us to "contribute to our goal [of seeing the Good]."

It is here that, with Burnyeat, I disagree with Broadie's claim that there is no
textual evidence for Plato holding that philosophical or ethical reasoning is, in
some sense, mathematical in nature. Indeed, not only does this supposition
answer the question of why mathematics is "good for the soul," but too it
answers why the mathematical branches are so ordered, with the mathematical
theory of harmony as the highest. This is because "concord" and "harmony,"
both mathematical and ethical, are to be accounted for by the metamathematical
use of geometric theory of proportion. Thus, we may finally conclude that
Plato's criticism of mathematics as currently practiced is not, as *part of* interpretations build their case on, that it makes use of hypotheses, rather it is that it is
taken to rely on sense perception, (e.g., the counting numbers of "tradesmen and
retailers in the case of theories of arithmetic, the "constructed diagrams and
figures" in the case of theories of geometry, the "ornaments of the heavens" in
the case of theories of astronomy, and the "audible concordances" in the case of
theories of cosmology). What we will next see is the way in which the geometrical theory of proportion plays its double role: as a mathematical theory of
cosmology and as a metamathematical theory of what measures harmony and
concord itself. It is this last use, when applied to the philosopher's forms, that
lends itself to the philosopher's inquiry into moral matters and, in so doing, gets
the philosopher closer to grasping the Good.

In what way, then, does the geometrical theory of proportion allow for the
organization of all other mathematical subjects so that we come to see what they
have in common, and just how does this relate the philosopher's goal of
grasping the Good? I will take up the details of answering this question in the
next section. For now, what I want to point out is that for *all* of these mathematical subjects it is mathematical practice that summons thought; that is, it is by
"making use of" or "ascending to" (531c) mathematical problems, and *not*
concerning ourselves, as current practitioners of mathematics do, with physical
or mathematical images, that we are motivated by the use of the faculty of
thought to move upward and so "*wake up* the understanding" (514d). Thus, even
when faced with overcoming the errors of current practitioners, Plato *does not*

require that the mathematician be so motivated by these mistakes to move even further upward toward adopting the philosopher's dialectical method and, in so doing, use the faculty of understanding to move into the realm of the forms. That is why Plato is careful to mention that "all these subjects are *merely preludes* to the theme [of attaining the good] itself" (531d; italics added); this is why Plato next takes time to remind us that we should

> *not* think that people who are clever in these [mathematical] matters *are dialecticians* ... [they] can *neither give an account nor approve one* [and so] cannot know *what any of the things are* that we say they must know.
> (531d–e; italics added)

Thus, Plato's mathematician is neither a dialectician nor can they know the forms: the mathematician's hypothesis are taken *as if* they were first principles, and, consequently, the mathematician's objects are taken *as if* they exist. To see that this is what Plato fully intends, we turn next to his *re*consideration the mathematician's ontology. That is, now making use of both the Cave analogy's distinction between being and becoming, and the proportions of the divided line, so that now the realm of being aligns to the intelligible and the realm of becoming aligns to the sensible, Plato tell us that

> the release from bonds and the turning around from shadows to statues and the light; and then the ascent out of the cave to the sun; and there the continuing inability to look directly at the animals, the plants, and the light of the sun, but instead at *divine reflections in water and shadows of things that are*, and not, as before, merely as shadows of statues thrown by another source of light, that when judged in relation to the sun, *is as shadowy as they –* all this practice of the crafts we mentioned [mathematics] *has the power to lead* the best part of the soul upward until it sees *the best among the things that are*, just as before the *clearest thing* in the body was to the brightest thing in the bodily and visible world. (532b–c; italics added)

So, in contrast to the philosopher's objects (the forms as "the best among the things that are" or the "clearest thing"), the mathematician's objects, while in the intelligible realm and so in the realm of being, are better than mathematical "images" (which are now taken as akin to physical images or shadows of physical things), but are still less clear than forms, and so themselves remain ontologically "shadowy." That is, while in the Divided Line mathematical images were taken as akin to physical images and mathematical objects them-selves were taken as akin to physical objects themselves, Book 7 ends with us taking mathematical objects as akin to shadowy physical images!!! So *re*con-sidered, the mathematician's objects are thus even more removed from the philosopher's forms!

When next pushed by Glaucon to "discuss it [the realm of the forms] in the same way as we did the prelude [as we did with mathematics]" and, in so doing, to further clarify "in what way the power of dialectical discussion works, into what kinds it is divided, and what road it follows" (532d; italics added), Socrates replies:

> Whether it is really so or not – that's not something on which it is any longer worth insisting. But that there is some such thing to be seen [the Good], that is something on which we must insist ... And mustn't we also insist that the power of dialectical discussion could reveal it only to someone experienced in the subjects we described, and cannot do so in any other way (533a).

Regardless, then, of "what kinds" the realm of forms is divided into, Plato insists on two things: that the Good exists and

> [a]t the very least, no one will dispute our claim by arguing that there is another road of inquiry [besides the mathematical one] that tries to acquire *a systematic and wholly general* grasp of what each thing itself is ... .
>
> (533b; italics added)

Having thus situated the necessary role of a mathematical education, Plato next takes the opportunity, again in light of the Cave analogy, to *re*consider the mathematician's method as

> ... *to some extent* grasping what is – I mean, geometry and the subjects that follow it. For we saw that while *they do dream about what is*, they *cannot see it while wide awake* as long as they make use of hypotheses that they *leave undisturbed*, and for which they cannot give any argument. After all, *when the first principle is unknown*, and the conclusion and the steps in between are put together out of what is unknown, what mechanism could possibly turn any agreement reached in such cases *knowledge*. (533b–c; italics added)

Importantly, and a point often missed in the interpretative literature, Plato, as a result of holding the mathematician's hypothetical method as *distinct from* the philosopher's, here *re*considers his use of the term "knowledge," reserving it for *philosophers only*.[38] That is, having *re*considered and further distinguished the mathematician's method from the philosopher's, Plato next turns to *re*consider his epistemological terms so that the mathematician, using hypothesis *as if* they were true first principles to solve a problem, has an understanding of their objects, but *not* knowledge!!

---

[38] Tait (2002), for example, misses this narrowing of the use of the term "knowledge" and, as a result, problematically collapses the distinction between the objects of the mathematician and the philosopher: "(t)he faculties explicitly mentioned there are opinion and knowledge. Since the Forms are clearly objects of knowledge ... " (p. 5).

> From force of habit, we have often called these branches knowledge. But they
> need another name, since they are *clearer than belief* and *darker than*
> *knowledge*. We distinguished them by the term "thought" somewhere before
> [in the Divided Line] ... It will be satisfactory, then, to do what we did before
> and call the first section *knowledge*, the second *thought*, the third *opinion*, and
> the fourth *imagination*. The last two together we call *belief*, the other two,
> *understanding*. (533d–534a; italics added)

What next follows is *the* crucial claim for my argument that mathematical
objects are *not* forms: as a result of these *re*considered methodological and
epistemological distinctions, Plato will now *re*consider the ontological status of
mathematical objects. They arise from the use of the hypothetical method and
not the dialectical method, and, as a consequence, they are *objects of thought*
and not *objects of knowledge*; they are "concerned with being" but are also
conjectural – that is, they are more akin to the "shadowy" objects of the
imagination. Again, by adding the Cave analogy to the divided line, we have
that just mathematical objects, as measured against physical images, are as
being is to becoming, so too mathematical objects, as measured against forms,
are *conjectured* objects[39] – that is, they are objects that we take *as if* they were
real for the purpose of solving a problem. That Plato intends this ontological
"akinness" is clear:

> Belief is concerned with becoming; understanding with being. And as being
> is to becoming, so understanding is to belief; and as understanding is to belief,
> so knowledge is to opinion and so *thought* to *imagination*.
>
> (534a; italics added)

Thus, bringing the Sun and the Cave analogies together, and using the ratios of
the clarity as set by the Divided Line analogy as markers of existence and truth,
we are left to conclude that mathematical objects are in the realm of the
intelligible and so are "concerned with being" (534a), but when compared to
objects of knowledge (i.e., to forms), mathematical objects, as objects of
thought – since thought is akin to imagination – are *not* forms, just as physical
images, as objects of imagination, are *not* physical objects. This explains the
sense in which the mathematician hypothesizes "the odd," "the even," "the
various figures"; but too once so hypothesized, they can then think about them
as if they existed, even if they cannot know they exist because they lack a first-
principled account of their being. This, then, is all Plato plans to say of the
matter of the distinction between mathematical and philosophical methods,

---

[39] Again, that this is the intended interpretation is further witnessed by Plato's invention the term
eikasai at 511e; he wants to use the manner in which this term is akin to both "imagine" and "to
guess at" to do analogical work when he comes to claim that just as the faculty of thought is akin
to the faculty of imagination so too are their objects.

their epistemic faculties, and their objects. And too this is all he is going to say about "the things" that each deals with:

> But as for *the ratios between the things these deal with*, and the division of either the believable or intelligible section into two, *let's pass them by* ... in case they involve us in accounts many times longer than the ones we have already gone through [lest it fill us up with many times more *arguments of ratios* than we have already[40]]. (534a; italics added)

This marks the point on which Burnyeat (2000) builds his interpretation of Plato's quietist stance of the "external" ontological status on mathematical objects.[41] This too is the point where Burnyeat and I fundamentally disagree. Burnyeat holds that "the things these deal with" is a reference to the distinction between mathematical and philosophical as intelligible kinds of things and so he considers the question that Plato intends to "pass by" the question of whether mathematical objects are forms, or intermediate kinds of things. Burnyeat says of this passage: "[t]o refuse to contemplate the result of dividing the objects on the intelligible section of the Line is to refuse to go into the distinction between the objects of mathematical thought and Forms" (p. 34).

It is this reading, moreover, that licenses Burnyeat's further claim that even if "internally," from within the context of *mathematical practice*, we can deny, as Burnyeat and I do, both that mathematical objects "could ultimately be derived from Forms" (p. 34) and "that Plato thinks mathematics is directly about Forms" (p. 35), we cannot, on this "internal" basis, get to the "external" metaphysical claim that mathematical objects are not forms, and so must ultimately rest quiet on the matter. And so, according to Burnyeat, we must conclude that the "external" question "is not discussed in the *Republic*" (p. 33). I disagree. Not only is this quietest view out of line, as Burnyeat himself notes, with the fact that the "external" question "was certainly debated in the Academy, as we can tell from the last two Books of Aristotle's *Metaphysics*" (p. 33), but, as I have shown, in both the Divided Line and Book 7 of the *Republic*,[42] Plato *has* shown us, both mathematically and philosophically that mathematical objects are not forms. Moreover, he has further shown us, in the *Meno*, the *Republic*, and the *Theaetetus*, that it does matter whether our mathematical "kinds of things" are proportioned in ratios that are geometric or arithmetic, so that the supposedly

---

[40] Here, in square brackets, I use Burnyeat's (2000) translation, which, as he notes (p. 34, n. 49), "plays on the mathematical and dialectical meaning of *logos*," these being "arguments of ratios" and "accounts," respectively.

[41] Note too that it is precisely here that Tait (2002) makes his case for taking mathematical objects as geometric forms: "[Plato] seems to be saying that both the domain of the sensibles and the domain of the Forms are to be subdivided ... [b]ut ... he leaves it aside ... " (p. 21). Again, I will show that this is *not* the question he leaves aside.

[42] For a diagrammatic summary of my interpretation, see my Divided Line (Figure 1).

"external" question of how mathematical "kinds of things" are ratioed *is* answered, and too it is answered "internally," – that is, is answered withing the context of mathematical practice by appealing to a mathematical theory not a metaphysical theory.

On my interpretation, what Plato is here "passing by" is the question of the ratios between the kinds of things in *each* of the mathematical and the philosophical realm. That is, he is not going to take up the question of how these mathematical kinds of objects should be taken as kinds proportioned by geometric ratios, by, for example, appealing to the specifics of Theodorus' developing theory, except to say that the geometric theory of proportion is the highest mathematical branch. Likewise, of the kinds of things that philosophy deals with, forms like Temperance, Justice, Good, and so on, he is not going to consider the question of how exactly these kinds of objects should be taken as kinds proportioned by the Good, by, for example, appealing to the Platonic notions of "participation" or "presence" or "imitation," except to say that the Good is the highest form. Note too that this reading is further in line with Socrates' dismissive reply (at 533a) to Glaucon's question of "into what kinds" the objects of understanding (i.e., the forms) are divided. He has already said he is not going to get into the discussion of "kinds of" forms; likewise, he is saying here that he is not going to get into the discussion of either "kinds of" mathematical objects or "kinds of" forms.

The last point that Plato does pause to make even more clear is that the differences in methodology *demand* differences in both epistemology and ontology. That is, while mathematics can be used to "grasp some image of the Good," because the mathematicians' method does not begin with first principles, it cannot offer an account "of the being" of mathematical objects, so they remain as objects of thought as opposed to objects of understanding (i.e., forms). To think otherwise, we are told, is simply irrational:

> So don't you too call someone a dialectician when he is able to *grasp an account of the being* of each thing? And when he cannot do so ... he *does not know it* ... Then the same applies to the Good. Unless some can give an account of the form of the Good ... striving to examine things *not in accordance with belief*, but *in accordance with being* ... And if he does manage to grasp some image of it, you will say that it is through *belief, not knowledge*, that he grasps it; that *he is dreaming and asleep* through his present life ... [so] even if you reared [your children by way of the method of mathematics] ... they are still *irrational* as the proverbial lines [as the lines so called in geometry].[43] (534b–d; italics added)

---

[43] Reeve notes that Plato here intends for a pun to be used: "*alogon* can mean "irrational" (as applied to people) and "incommensurable" (as applied to line in geometry)" (p. 230, n. 24).

Plato here tells us of the limits of a mathematical education: the mathematical method, in so far as it reasons down from hypotheses *as if* they were first principles, as opposed to reasoning up from hypothesis to first principles, cannot grasp "the being of each thing," whether that thing is a mathematical thing or a philosophical thing, like the Good. But, nonetheless, and importantly, the benefit of a mathematical education on the philosopher-in-training is that mathematics can be used to "grasp some image of the Good." In the next section, I will consider the question of how this is possible. For now, I pause to remind the reader that Plato intends the geometrical theory of proportion to play a *metamathematical* role and, in the next section, I will show that Plato intends for this metamathematical role to be akin to the *metaphilosophical* role played by the Good. What we will see is that the geometrical theory of proportion plays a double mathematical role: as a *mathematical* theory of cosmology and as the highest, or *metamathematical,* theory that accounts for the concord and harmony (i.e., for the good order) among all the branches of mathematics. Next, using proportional reasoning to take this role as akin to the role of the Good we come to see the sense in which the Good, as the highest form, accounts for the good order among the forms. It is this use of proportional reasoning, now applied to the philosopher's forms, that lends itself to the philosopher's inquiry into moral matters and, in so doing, gets the philosopher closer to grasping the Good. But, while the mathematician's method can be used to account for mathematical objects (e.g., for irrational numbers) it cannot be used to make mathematicians rational – that is, it cannot be used to account "for the being" of either mathematical or philosophical objects, and as such the philosopher, whose goal is to reach the Good, will need another method.

As I have hinted at, and will now argue, one should see Plato's entire account of mathematics as an attempt to move past any metamathematical use of the Pythagorean arithmetical theory of proportion so that he can include those "irrationals" that have a *logos*, or have an account in terms of geometric ratios; for example, those numbers that can be given an account of by a geometric theory of proportion.[44] As we are shown in the *Meno*, some irrational lengths,

---

I agree entirely that this is Plato's intention, which is why I prefer Shorey's translation, which explicitly mentions geometry.

[44] Again, see Fowler (2003) for an account of the difference between a geometric and an arithmetic theory of proportion; see especially p. 26, where he has his Socrates claim that Eudoxus' geometrical theory, even though it is not *fully* developed, is to be preferred to Archytas' arithmetical theory, because "their approach does not allow them to describe all ratios that can occur in geometry." Balashov (1994) disagrees both with the assumption that the theory of proportion needs be geometrical and too that Eudoxus' theory was a geometrical theory; his references are Dreher (1990) and Sayre (1983) respectively. See also Balashov (1994) for an investigation of whether, by adopting a geometrical account, we can argue that the divided line is intended to be proportioned in golden ratio (as first suggested by Brumbaugh [1954]) and a

which are constructed from the problem of doubling the length of the side of a two-foot square, are to be included as numbers qua objects of thought, because an account of them can be given in terms of geometrically ratioed lengths (e.g., as ratios measured by the diagonal of a two-foot square). To see that Plato further intends this metamathematical role to apply to all the branches of mathematics, we first recall his criticism of Pythagorean arithmetical accounts of astronomy and cosmology and next we recall that both Plato and Theaetetus were students of Theodorus, who was known to be developing a geometric theory of proportion that was aimed to account for all the branches of mathematics. This metamathematical use is further witnessed in the *Theaetetus* (145c–d) where Theaetetus tells Socrates that he learned all of arithmetic, geometry, astronomy, and harmonics from his teacher Theodorus, who is an expert (145a) in all of these subjects, and who, Socrates further tells us,

> was proving to us something about square roots, namely, that the sides (or roots) of squares representing three square feet and five square feet are not commensurable in length with the line representing one foot, and he went on in this way, taking all the separate cases up to the root of seventeen square feet. There for some reason he stopped. Now it occurred to us, since the number of square roots appeared to be unlimited, *to try to gather them into one class*, by which we could henceforth describe all the roots. (147d; italics added)

And, more importantly for my claim that his geometrical theory was known to Plato, note that just after this, when Theaetetus is asked by Socrates whether he has "found such a class," Theaetetus replies, "I think *we* did," and proceeds to sketch his account of numbers as geometrically proportioned measures, whereby "all numbers can be divided into two classes ... all the lines which form the plane figure representing the equilateral number we defined as *lengths*, while those which form the sides of squares equal in area to the oblongs we called *roots*, as not being commensurable with the others in length." Just after this Theaetetus tells us that "there is another distinction of the same sort in the case of solid geometrical figures and harmonics" (*Theaetetus*, 147e–148b).

So, while Tait (2002) rightly notes that Plato was "concerned with foundations because of the discovery of incommensurable line segments" (pp. 19–20), he is wrong to presume that the only "foundation" that can be given is one founded on the philosopher's dialectical method and an ontology of forms. Simply, the geometric theory of proportion is taken as the theory that answers the metamathematical question of what theory accounts for "the ratios between

---

discussion of whether the divided line should be constructed vertically or horizontally; for my purposes, I leave these debates to the side.

the things" of the various branches of mathematics. So, against all *part of* interpretations, no metaphysical move to the philosopher's dialectical method is needed to answer this metamathematical question. Again, against Cornford, White, Benson, Tait, *and* Burnyeat, this question is an internal mathematical question, that is, while Plato does not take up the question of exactly how the kinds of objects in the mathematical realm are ratioed, as we are clearly shown in the *Theaetetus*, it is nonetheless a question that he intends to be settled *by mathematicians*, like Theaetetus and Theodorus. It is neither a question that requires the use of the philosopher's dialectical method, and so requires mathematical objects as geometric or metaphysical forms, nor is it an "external" one that is passed over in silence.

5 The Good in Mathematics

How, then, does the learning of mathematics, and, in particular, the metamathematical "investigation of all the subjects we have mentioned," so that it "arrives at what they share in common with one another and what their affinities are, and draws conclusions about their kinship," "contribute something" to philosopher's goal of grasping the Good? To answer this question, we must first answer the question: What is the relationship between mathematical reasoning and philosophical/moral reasoning?. Here my aim will be to show, against Broadie and in agreement with Burnyeat, that Plato *does* intend for philosophical inquiry to be modeled on mathematical inquiry. But too, against Burnyeat and in agreement with Broadie, this not because the realm of forms is itself mathematically structured, rather it is that our reasoning about both the good in mathematics and the Good in philosophy are to be founded on *proportional reasoning*. Thus, to answer these questions, I now turn to consider "the good" in mathematics and, in this light, further investigate the *philosophical role* of the geometric theory of proportion. Recall the discussion that underpins both the Divided Line and Book 7: how the philosopher is to reach the Good. Recall too that Socrates introduces the Divided Line analogy to explain the Sun's analogical claim that "what the latter (the good) is in the intelligible realm in relation to understanding and intelligible things, the former (the Sun) is in the visible realm in relation to sight and visible things" (508c). Bringing the Sun and Divided Line analogies together, we are then guided to construct the *geometrically ratioed* divided line under the assumption that the Sun is "sovereign" over the visible and the good is "sovereign" over the intelligible (509e).

Moreover, it is just this assumption that allows us to use the notion of clarity to proportion the ratios of the sub-realms of both the physical and the intelligible realms (i.e., the Sun makes images and physical objects clear to the same degree or proportion that the good makes mathematical objects and forms clear). Moreover, in the visible realm, it is the Sun that ratios the degree of clarity (508b), and, as a result, physical objects and physical images respectively relate, on the basis of the ratios of their clarity or opacity, *ontologically* to existence and nonexistence, and *epistemically* to truth and untruth. Analogously, it is the good that ratios the degree of clarity in the intelligible sub-realms to the same degree or proportion as the Sun ratios of the visible sub-realms. As a result, philosophical objects (forms) and mathematical objects respectively relate, on the basis of the ratios of their clarity or opacity, *ontologically* to existence and nonexistence, and *epistemically* to truth and untruth. Next, adding the ratios as set by the analogy of the Cave, mathematical objects relate to philosophical objects in the same ratio as physical images relate to physical objects, so that mathematical objects are *akin to* objects of imagination – that is, they are less real (they are "shadowy" [532b]) than philosophical objects, and the statements about them are less true than philosophical statements ("they are clearer than belief but darker than knowledge" [533d]).

So far, I have merely summed the claims I have considered. Now I will further argue that the geometrical theory of proportion plays an additional role in the mathematical sub-realm, and this role is intended to be taken as *akin to* the role played by the Good in the philosophical sub-realm. Indeed, this is the reason why the philosopher-in-training must take up the study of mathematics for *ten years* and why they must proceed from arithmetic, to geometry, to solid geometry, to solids in motions, to the harmony of such motions, and end at the geometrical theory of proportion itself. Only then will they come to see the double role that it plays, both as a mathematical theory of cosmology and as a metamathematical foundation that accounts for the good order of the various branches of mathematics. Finally, it is by appreciating this last role that they are further able to understand the analogous role that the Good itself plays in accounting for the good order of the forms.

Until recently, there has been little discussion in the literature as to why Plato orders his mathematical subjects in the manner he does.[45] To this end, I now turn to consider why it is that the *geometrical* theory of proportion is the last, and I

---

[45] Notable exceptions are, of course, Burnyeat (2000), and too Miller (1999) and Zoller (2007). See, for example, Zoller's suggestion that

> mathematical training provides the dialectician with a reward that goes beyond simple mental exercise; this privilege is the opportunity to study proportion, the understanding of which is the second mathematical ability required for understanding the hierarchy of Forms. *Proportion is the most important aspect of mathematics for the future dialectician.* This is certainly reflected in the order of the five mathematical studies that Plato prescribes in his curriculum, which culminates in the study of harmonics.
>
> (p. 62; italics added)

hold, the highest, mathematical subject. Recall that in his discussion of the theory of harmony, Plato claims that this subject has two uses. The first use is as an "indispensable aid" in the philosophers' "search for the beautiful and the good" (531c); for this use, Burnyeat (2000, p. 34) is right that the discussion of the "ratios between the things these deal with" (534a), is beside the point of Socrates' message. However, as noted, he is wrong to assume that this reference is to "the things" that mathematics and philosophy deal with, and, as a result, he is wrong to conclude that Plato adopts a metaphysical quietist position as regards "the distinction between the objects of mathematical thought and Forms" (534a). Against both Burnyeat and Broadie's quietism, what I have demonstrated thus far is that Plato *has* considered, in the Divided Line and in Book 7, this metaphysical distinction, and *has* shown that mathematical objects are *not* forms.

As I have argued, what Plato has refused to explicitly discuss is the ratios between the things that *each of* mathematics and philosophy deals with. But, as noted, in the mathematical sub-realm, he, following Theodorus and Theaetetus, for example, will need to do this when he comes to consider the second use of the theory of proportion: the "investigation of *all* the [mathematical] subjects we have mentioned" with the aim of arriving at "*what they share in common* with one another and what their affinities are, and *drawing conclusions about their kinship*" (531d). Thus, in the mathematical sub-realm, what the geometric theory of proportion does is provide a metamathematical good ordering of the branches of mathematics and, in so doing, provides an overarching account of what all the mathematical subjects share in common. However, it does not do this by standing above, or apart from, the other mathematical subjects, rather it is constitutive of what they all have in common – that is, the geometric conception of ratio – and it is in virtue of this, that it provides an overarching account of the all the kinds of mathematical objects in terms of geometric ratios. That is, grasping this metamathematical role allows us to "ascend to problems" by providing an overarching account of the "ratios between the things" that mathematics deals with. For example, as seen from the view provided by the geometric theory of proportion, the "kinds of things" of arithmetic (i.e., numbers) are *not* to be understood as Pythagorean arithmetical indivisible units;[46]

Where we differ, however, is that she sees mathematical objects as, or composed out of, proportioned forms so that "the objects both of dianoia and of noesis are the Forms" (p. 46). See also Fowler (2003), Robins (1995), and Miller (1999) for differing critical analyses of the view that Plato intends the theory of proportion to, in some sense, underlie all of the other mathematical subjects.

[46] I note here that the "numbers as, or as composed of, indivisible units" view is the standard reading of several interpreters of Plato. Typically, such views are born out of the view that mathematical objects are forms. While I cannot here give the full argument for the claim that for

rather, they are to be understood as geometrical measures. More importantly, as measures of geometric ratios, as Plato himself demonstrates in the *Meno*, their rationality or irrationality is not decided on the basis of whether such measures are arithmetically commensurable or not, but rather by whether they can, in light of a geometric theory of proportion, be *given an account* in terms of the ratios of their geometrically constructed measures. Again, going back to the *Meno*, the length of the side that doubles the area of a two-foot long[47] square, while incommensurable, is nonetheless "rational" in so far as an account of it can be given in terms of the ratio of the proportions of the sides (in terms of the length of the diagonal as set by the Pythagorean theorem) when the length of the two-foot side is taken as a measure.[48]

This interpretation of the geometric theory of proportion as both account-giving and constitutive of the subject matter of mathematics is not only important for understanding what Plato takes arithmetic numbers and geometric figures to be, but for understanding the account-giving role of the Good as well. That is, the Good, in so far as it serves an analogous role in the philosophical realm as the geometric theory of proportion in the mathematical realm, does not stand above, or apart from, the other forms; rather, it too by being a measure is constitutive of "ratios between the things" that metaphysics deals with – that is, the ratios between the forms themselves. These account-giving and constitutive roles of the good, in both the mathematical and the philosophical sub-realms, are further in agreement with the Greek notion of *logos* as not only something that merely provides an account or order but also something that provides a *good order*, that is, an order that establishes both concord and

---

Plato numbers are not to be taken as arithmetical indivisible units, but rather as geometric measures, I first point the reader to consider both *Republic* (524b–526b), where he argues against taking numbers as "counting units," and *Theaetetus* (147d–148b), where he argues for taking them as geometric measures. Second, I rely on Fowler's (2003) interpretation of the mathematics of Plato's Academy as being founded on a geometric theory of proportion. Third, I note that Eudoxus, who was a student of Plato and, indeed, was head of the Academy, was also focused on developing a geometric theory of proportion that would underpin astronomy, solid geometry, *and* arithmetic. Finally, I note that Burnyeat, despite our differences, also shares this interpretation of number: "notice that the unit is represented ... by a line ... not by a point ... to suppose that the divisibility of the line ... has significance in an arithmetical context ... is to confuse arithmetical with geometrical division in the most laughable way" (pp. 30–31).

[47] This distinction between numbers as arithmetical units versus geometrical measures is further witnessed in Plato's use of a *two*-foot square. That is, he could have easily chosen a one-foot square to make his point, but this would have allowed for the interpretation of numbers as composed of indivisible units (e.g., of one as *the* indivisible unit out of which the other numbers are composed). By choosing a two-foot square, he is telling his reader that a number is whatever makes a geometrical measure, so in this case the two-foot length is the number that makes the measure of the length of the side.

[48] That Plato wants us to keep this example in mind is evidenced by his mention of "the diagonal itself" (510d–e).

harmony.[49] Finally, we must also note that implicit in the Greek notion of an account as a good order is always a moral, or value-laden, component. It is in all of these senses of "good," then, that we are to understand why a mathematical education is not only necessary for the philosopher's education but also good for the philosopher's soul.[50] That is, it is only when we place our focus on the metamathematical account-giving role of the geometric theory of proportion that the study of the various mathematical subjects can be used to "redirect the soul from its downward journey to its upward one," so that the philosopher comes to see that, analogously,[51] "the *last thing* to be seen is the form of the Good" (517c; italics added). It is this analogy, then, that allows us to see why the mathematician's metamathematical investigation into the "ratios between kinds of things" that mathematics deals with "contributes something" to the philosopher's goal of grasping the Good.

It is now time to consider Burnyeat's (2000) interpretation of this second, metamathematical, use of theory of proportion and his further claim that it is constitutive of the "kinds of things" that metaphysics deals with, so that philosophical dialectic itself is the metamathematical attempt to account for all hypotheses, this with the more than confusing claim that Plato "leaves us to infer that dialectical debate about the conceptual foundations of mathematics itself … is a debate about values like justice" (p. 46). Thus, in the philosopher's accounting for their hypotheses in terms of forms, as Burnyeat explains, they

---

[49] If, for example, we accept that the divided line is to be proportioned both geometrically and harmoniously, and if we consider that the Greek *sine qua non* for harmony was the golden ratio, then we might argue that the divided line ought to be proportioned according to the golden ratio. Again, see Balashov (1994), for an overview of this debate. Moreover, we note too that the notion of *logos* is also connected, and quite explicitly so in Plato's *Timaeus*, to the astronomical notion of *kosmos*; here the theory of proportion does the cosmological work of well-ordering the world in terms of the ratios between the various geometric solids, constructed from the initial solid triangle, such that, "the *ratio* of their (particles of earth, air, fire and water) numbers, motions, and other properties, everywhere God, as far as necessary allowed or gave consent, has exactly perfected and *harmonized* in due *proportion*" (*Timaeus* 56c; italics added). See also Burnyeat (2000; especially pp. 51–68), for a discussion of the role of proportion in the *Timaeus*.

[50] See Burnyeat's claim that "(m)athematics and dialectic are good for the soul, not only because they give you understanding of objective value, but also because in so doing they fashion justice and temperance with wisdom in your soul. They make all the difference to the way you think about values in practice" (p. 77). See also Kung's (1987) claim that only the study of mathematics can teach us "the ratios and proportions among the [parts of the soul] that constitute virtue" (p. 332).

[51] That Plato intends this analogy between the account-giving role of the geometric theory of proportion and the account-giving role of the Good, is also evidenced by Socrates' request in the *Theaetetus* (148b–d), that Theaetetus "take as a model your answer about [numbers as geometrically measured] roots … to find a single formula that applies to the many kinds of knowledge" (148d), where the single formula they come to consider is knowledge as true belief that is tethered by an account. This too might give evidence against Balashov's (1994) claim (see p. 292) that the "justified true belief" account of knowledge cannot be used to analyse the account of knowledge in the *Republic*, this despite its obvious use in analyses of mathematical knowledge in both the *Meno* and the *Theaetetus*.

will, along the way, need to also account for the mathematician's hypotheses likewise in terms of forms:

> [T]he future rulers will not go on to their five years' dialectic until they have achieved a synoptic view of all the mathematical disciplines … and dialectic will centre on explaining the hypotheses of mathematics in a way that mathematics does not, and cannot, do … They [philosophers] will stop taking mathematical hypotheses as starting-points and try to account for them in terms of Forms. (pp. 27–38)

Clearly, I disagree. Where, however, do we part ways? Burnyeat and I agree that this "synoptic view" comes by way of the use of the theory of proportion itself. That is, once the mathematician, after their ten years of study, comes to this view of the account-giving role of the theory of proportion, they then, for another fifteen years, have to apply this role of proportion itself to practical matters (matters concerning the proportioning of both military matters and matters of state administration; see 539e–540a). Only then are they in position to aim, for the next five years, to become a philosopher by applying this account-giving role of proportion to metaphysical matters (matters concerning the proportion-ing of the forms, ethical matters, and even matters concerning the proportioning of the soul). Were we differ is that for Burnyeat, after the philosopher has grasped the Good as the highest form, they must then turn to give an account of the *good order* of both mathematical and metaphysical matters in terms of forms, then, as a philosopher king, to matters concerning the good order of the city, its citizens, and themselves (534a–b). Thus, Burnyeat's (2000) answer to his question – "Is the study of mathematics merely instrumental to knowledge of the Good, in Plato's view, or is the content of mathematics a *constitutive part* of ethical understanding?" (p. 6; italics added) – is:

> For present purposes, it is enough that *dialectic is described in terms that suggest what we might call a metamathematical inquiry.* The education of rulers is mathematical, in once sense or another, *all the way to the top* … mathematics is the route to knowledge of the Good because it is a *constitutive* part of ethical understanding … philosophers will think of the mathematical structures they internalize on the way up as abstract schemata for applying their knowledge of the Good in the social world.
>
> (pp. 46–73; italics added)

Here I stand with Broadie (2020) that making the metamathematical debate about the foundations of mathematics a dialectical debate leads to "idiocy of demanding that mathematics should model itself on ethical philosophizing" (p. 23). Ok, perhaps not idiocy, but at least inconsistency: the assumption that the metaphysical realm of forms is itself mathematically structured and the subsequent appeal to an account- giving role of forms for mathematics is clearly inconsistent with Burnyeat's stated quietism. Burnyeat has it that at a mathematical level the mathematician and the philosopher's methods are distinct but that at the metamathematical level only the philosopher can account for the good order of mathematics. Simply, Burnyeat has gone too far, both in claiming that mathematics is constitutive of ethical understanding and, consequently, that at least one task of the philosopher is to dialectically account for mathematical hypotheses in terms of forms. Where has Burnyeat gone wrong? As noted, the first error is that he has taken the theory of proportion as constitutive of ethical inquiry, leading to the view that dialectic itself is a metamathematical activity, so that the good order of mathematics is to be accounted for by a philosophical investigation into the good order of the forms. The second is that he takes his metamathematical theory of proportion as arithmetical as opposed to as geometrical.

Again, on my interpretation *only* the geometrical theory of proportion can contribute to the goal of allowing both the mathematician and the philosopher to grasp the good. As regards Burnyeat first error, mathematics does not need philosophy, either its method of dialectic or its ontology of forms, to account for it's good order. As I have demonstrated, the theory of geometrical proportion is not just a metamathematical theory, it is the highest mathematical theory (i.e., the theory that good orders all of the branches of mathematics). And too in this role it is to be taken as akin to the Good as the highest form that good orders all of the forms. That is, the metamathematical role of the geometric theory of proportion is to be taken as akin to the *metaphilosophical* role played by the Good; each is constitutive of "ratios between the things these deal with." So it is by analogy, and not by constitution, that we are to understand the metaphilosophical use of the proportional reasoning. That Burnyeat has missed this point is a result of his second error. As I have argued, taking the route offered by the Pythagorean arithmetical theory of Archytas will be "labor in vain," because it simply cannot play this metamathematical account-giving role, and so cannot be used to run the intended analogy between the theory of proportion as the highest theory and the Good as the highest form. According to Burnyeat's (2000) reading, which uses Archytas' arithmetical theory of proportion to take "all five mathematical subjects as 'sister sciences'" (p. 19),[52] "from Plato's standpoint, Archytas' fault would be his developing such a mathematics merely in order to explain, *from above as it were*, the auditory experiences we enjoy" (p. 53; italics added).

---

[52] As Burnyeat (2000, pp. 15–16) explains, Archytas held astronomy and harmonics as "sister sciences" while, Philolaus, like Tait, took geometry as "the mother-city."

In contrast, I hold that, besides Archytas' reliance "auditory concordances," both Archytas and Burnyeat's fault is that they ought to have taken the theory of proportion as both geometrical and as a Philolausean "mother-city." That is, if this metamathematical theory is to fulfill the mathematician's goal of good ordering the branches of mathematics and, in so doing, aiding in the philosopher's grasping of the Good as the highest form, it needs to be taken as the highest theory. Indeed, that Burnyeat takes the theory of proportion as arithmetical, or minimally, that, in nodding to Archytas, he fails to distinguish between the two accounts, is what gets him into the problem of having to explain the order of the mathematical subjects:

> The snag is … [the fifth subject] mathematical harmonics. That *seems to presuppose and build upon arithmetic* rather than astronomy, its immediate predecessor in the preferred order. Harmonics, though mathematically simpler than advanced geometry and astronomy, is the first discipline to take ratio itself as the primary object of study. (p. 73; italics added)

My reading avoids this "snag": the geometric theory of proportion is last in order of education because of the double role it plays: as the theory that accounts for the concord and harmony of the cosmos, and as the highest theory that accounts for the concord and harmony of the various branches of mathematics in terms of ratios. What Burnyeat has failed to consider is that, after their study of the five mathematical subjects, the mathematician must "ascend to problems" and come to metamathematically see that the *good order* of mathematics will be the one that puts the geometric, as opposed to the arithmetic, theory of proportion last in order of education but also first in order of account.[53]

Thus, I disagree entirely, with Burnyeat's claim that

> Plato was never in a position to tell grown-up mathematicians what to do or not do, any more that he could (or would) tell grown-up philosophers what to believe … The educational curriculum of the *Republic* is designed to produce future rulers in an ideal city, not to confine research in real-life Athens to subjects that will lead to knowledge of the Good. (p. 17, n. 23)

As I have demonstrated, Plato is telling both mathematicians and philosophers what they need to do to grasp the good. During their ten years of mathematical study, from within the pedagogical context of discovery, they are to *work up* from arithmetic, to geometry, to solid geometry, to solid geometry in motion, to the harmony of such motions, and then they are to "ascend" to the geometric

---

[53] Another snag, then, of taking the "sister sciences" view is it cannot distinguish between the last in order or education and the first in order of account uses of the theory of proportion because the branches themselves are taken as "a family … in which the prior and simpler provides the basis for a series of more and more elaborate developments" (p. 68).

theory of proportion as the highest theory. Then, starting from there, now from within the mathematical context of justification, that is, the context that gives the account, they are to *work down* having grasped the overarching good ordering or account-giving role of the theory of proportion for all the kinds of mathematical objects in terms of geometric ratios. Likewise, during their fifteen years of philosophical study, from within the pedagogical context of discovery, they are to *work up* from proportional reasoning to an account of "all the kinds" of philosophical objects in terms of their ratios (i.e., from the proportionality of military matters and matters of state administration to an account of the proportionality of forms to an account of the Good as the highest form). Then, starting from there, now from within the philosophical context of justification, for the next five years they are to work down having grasped the overarching good-ordering, account-giving, role of the Good. Thus, in as much as Plato is setting out how one is to become a good philosopher (i.e., a philosopher who aims to grasp the account-giving role of the Good), he is also setting out how one is to become a good mathematician (i.e., a mathematician who aims to grasp the account-giving role of the geometrical theory or proportion). In neither case, however, is there a need for the mathematician to adopt the philosopher's dialectical method and seek an account of their hypotheses in terms of forms; simply, the account of mathematics is given by a mathematical theory, not by a metaphysical one! So, against Burnyeat's (2000) claim that Plato's philosophers in training

> are not preparing to be professional mathematicians; nothing is said about making creative contributions to the subjects. Their ten years will take them to the synoptic view [as grasped by the theory of proportion], but they then switch to dialectic and philosophy. (p. 2)

I have shown that, in the *Republic*, the mathematician qua philosopher-in-training can certainly come to see the account-giving role of the geometric theory of proportion and its *akinness* to the account-giving role of the Good, without having to "make creative contributions" and this is why they can "pass by" the question of the "the ratios between the things these deal with." The mathematician, however, will have to concern themselves with this question; as Plato's repeated appeals to mathematicians like Theaetetus and Theodorus show, he does intend for this work to be taken up by mathematicians and not by philosophers. Thus, there is no need for the mathematician to "switch to dialectic and philosophy."

Recall that even though the mathematician, in their use the geometric theory of proportion, can come to give an account of their mathematical beliefs, they, nonetheless, in contrast to the philosopher, remain "irrational," or *alogos*, or *without* an account, because, as Plato explains, they examine things "in accordance with belief," whereas the philosopher examines things "in accordance with being." That is, the geometrical theory of proportion accounts for, or justifies, our beliefs about what we think numbers, squares, and son on are, but it cannot, in so doing, justify that they exist "in accordance with being." Only those things that are accounted for by the Good itself, as "the best among the things *that are*" – forms like Truth, Knowledge, Beauty, Virtue, and so on – can properly be said to exist "in accordance with being" – that is, can be *accounted for* by the Good itself.[54] Thus, the goal of a mathematical education is that, when aimed at philosophers in training, they come to understand that, in a sense analogous to the account-giving role played by the geometrical theory of proportion, the Good, as the highest form, accounts for what exists: it does not stand above, or apart from, the other forms, rather it is constitutive of what they have in common, and in virtue of this, the Good provides an overarching account of the being of those other "kinds of things" that are forms.[55]

We are now in position to measure my interpretation against Broadie's. As I have shown, there is certainly textual evidence that Plato argues for, and, indeed, wants us to conclude that philosophical inquiry is to be modelled on mathematical inquiry. On my reading this is because they are to be taken as *akin* in the sense that both are to be taken as being founded on proportional reasoning itself. How, then, is this all important proportional reasoning, aimed at grasping the good in mathematics and the Good philosophy, supposed to work? Especially given that the details of "the ratios between the things these deal with" with are "passed by"? In contrast with *part of* interpretations, it is not making mathematical inquiry part of philosophy inquiry. Yet too, it is neither, as Burnyeat would have it, by making dialectic itself a metamathematical inquiry. In contrast to both views, the answer to this question is found in Plato's presentation of the divided line itself. Plato has demonstrated the use and

---

[54] This is why, for example, Knowledge and Truth are "goodlike" but neither of them "is the good," because the Good is what *accounts for* the goodness of each, while, it itself, is yet more honored" (508e–509b). See also Zoller's (2007) claim that "the Forms are said to owe their existence and being known to the Good (509b) ... the Good is superior in rank and power to the Form of Being" (p. 63).

[55] See, for example, Zoller's (2007) claim that

proportion is important for understanding the blending of the Forms because of the hierarchical structure of the realm of Forms, meaning that the Forms closest to the top of the hierarchy (e.g., the Form of Justice, the Form of Beauty, the Form of Being) will be more blended with the Form of the Good than are the other Forms with which the Good is blended (e.g., the Form of a Dog and the Form of Bed), ... In the *Republic* Plato upholds the Form of the Good as the *arche*; ... As such the first principle (the Form of the Good) is what provides the structure for the hierarchy of Forms, the structure of reality and Being itself. (pp. 63–64)

value of such proportional reasoning, as built up out of the ratios the divided line, by *using it as an argument scheme it on us!*[56]

The Divided Line and the divided line of Book 7, as reconsidered in light of both the Sun and Cave analogies, shows us the value of the use of proportional reasoning made on the basis of geometric ratios. That is, the divided line itself, is constructed proportionally on the basis of the geometric ratios of the lines,[57] without telling us what those ratios are; it is the proportions, between both the ratioed sections and the ratioed subsections of the line itself, that allows us to follow Plato's proportional reasoning. And, in so doing, we arrive at what the Sun, the Divided Line, the Cave, and Book 7 "share in common with one another and what their affinities are" and next to use the analogies between these, for example, the akinness between the good-ordering role of the theory of proportion and the good-ordering role of the Good, to "draw conclusions about their kinship." By placing the mathematical theory of proportion as the highest metamathematical theory and the Good as the highest metaphilosophical form, Plato is showing us that even though their methods are distinct, metaphysical/ moral reasoning is to be taken as akin to mathematical reasoning. Not only does this supposition answer of why the mathematical branches are so ordered, again with the metamathematical theory of proportion itself as the highest theory, but too it answers the question of why the study of mathematics is good for the soul, namely, because the "concord" and "harmony," or the good order, of both the objects of the branches of mathematics and the objects of philosophy are to be accounted for by proportional reasoning. So, while the metaphysical/moral realm is not structured by mathematics per se, the proportional structure of the realm of forms is to be taken as akin to the proportional structure of the realm of mathematical objects in the sense that the good order of the forms themselves is to be accounted for by reasoning based on the mathematical notion of proportion.

Finally, and most importantly for my aim of showing that Plato was not a mathematical Platonist, the appeal to the *reconsidered* divided line on the basis of what the Sun, the Divided Line, the Cave, and Book 7 "share in common with

---

[56] I thank Patrick Maynard, my ancient philosophy professor while a graduate student at Western Ontario, for pushing me to always ask the question: What is Plato asking of us, as the reader, to do?.

[57] As noted, there is debate as to whether the divided line itself should be constructed arithmetically, such that the ratios are rationals, or geometrically, such that the ratios may be irrational. Again, see Balashov (1994) for a well-considered and extensive overview of this debate, including the question of whether the proportions of the line are in golden ratio. Textually, it appears as though both interpretations are possible; however, as I hope to have shown, once one appreciates the account-giving role of the geometric theory of proportions, it seems clear (I hope!) that Plato intends for the proportions of his divided line to be geometric and so measure both rational *and* irrational ratios.

one another and what their affinities are," when now aimed at the distinction between the ontology and epistemology of the realms and sub-realms, allows us, by use of proportional reasoning based on the ratios between the realms and sub-realms, to "draw conclusions about their kinship." Thus, we come to Plato's final proportional argument that

> as being is to becoming, so understanding is to belief; and as understanding is to belief, so knowledge is to belief [opinion] and so *thought* to *imagination*. (534a)

It is this proportional argument, taken in the context of the *re*considered geometric ratios of the lines, that allow us, as the reader, to reach the conclusion that the objects of mathematics are more akin *to* the objects of imagination then they are to those of knowledge. What Plato has shown us, through his geometrically structured proportional reasoning, is that mathematical objects, as objects of understanding, are "concerned with being." But too, as objects of thought, wherein thought is taken akin to imagination, they are more "shadowy" than philosophical objects, as objects of knowledge. Thus, he has shown us that because the method of mathematics is distinct from the method of philosophy, so too must be both the epistemological state of their understanding and ontological status of their objects. So, using proportional reasoning based on the *re*considered geometric ratios of the lines, we are now justified in "drawing a conclusion about their kinship": mathematical objects are distinct from forms.

6 Mathematics Versus Metaphysics

We now in a position to reconsider, at the level of the practice of mathematics, the typical mathematical Platonist components and to conclude that Plato was *not* a mathematical Platonist. Recall, then, the first component – that mathematical objects, as Platonic forms, exist independently of us in some metaphysical realm of forms. As I hope I have shown, for Plato, mathematical objects do not exist independently of us; they are conjectured objects and so they *depend* on the mathematical problem that we are attempting to solve. It is the problem at hand that gives rise to the needed hypotheses that we take as if they were first principles, and it is these together that give rise to the needed objects of thought, that we take as if they were real, and it is both that underwrite the arguments that we think we need to reach a given conclusion. Mathematical objects, then, exist in a methodological sense *not* in a metaphysical sense. As we have seen, in mathematics, existence is a consequence of truth – that is, is a consequence of taking our hypotheses *as if* they were true first principles for the purpose of solving a problem. In philosophy, by contrast, truth is a consequence of existence, that is, is a consequence of our tethering the truth of our hypotheses to independently existing forms. We next consider component (b), that the way things are in the metaphysical realm fixes the truth of mathematical statements. What we note, is that what fixes the truth of a mathematical statement is the mathematicians' method, not any philosophical or mathematical metaphysics; it is the demonstration of the conclusion, given the hypotheses and objects of thought that we begin within the context of a given problem, that fixes the truth of a mathematical statement. Finally, we reconsider component (c), that we come to know such truths by, somehow or other, "recollecting" the way things are in the meta-physical realm. For Plato, at least in the *Republic*, there is no need for recollection; we simply assume that we have the capacity for such under-standing, and we show that we come to understand such truths by our use of the method of hypothesis, which requires only that we can think of the object itself, that is, think of it *as if* it was independent of any mathematical diagram or figure. Mathematical understanding, then, is neither the result of our *discovering* the way things are in a metaphysical realm, nor our *creating* the way things are in our mind or in a community;[58] it is result of what we can *demonstrate* in the context of a given problem via the use of the hypoth-eses and objects we begin with. It is these considerations, that arise by keeping distinct the mathematician and the philosopher's methods, that allow us to see that Plato's practicing mathematician was a methodological realist *not* a metaphysical realist.

Next we come to reconsider, now at the level of the philosophy of mathemat-ics, the desire to solve those metamathematical problems concerning "into what kinds of things [mathematics] is divided" and "what road it follows" by providing an *overarching good ordering* or *an organizational account* of all of the mathematical subjects. What Plato shows us is that, from a metamathe-matical standpoint, to "undertake an investigation of all the mathematical subjects we have mentioned" and "arrive at what they share in common with one another so that we can draw conclusions about their kinship" we *do not* have to turn to philosophy. We do not have to turn to the dialectical method and a metaphysics of philosophical or geometrical forms; rather, we can turn to mathematics itself and use the geometric theory of proportion as the highest

---

[58] The objectivity of mathematical knowledge, then, is not explained by reference *stable objects*, like forms, but this does not mean that it is either subjective or socially constructed. Rather, objectivity is fixed by the *stability* of mathematical definitions. Here I point to Burnyeat's (2000) claim that "mathematical objects can only be grasped through precise definition, not otherwise, so there is good sense in the idea that precision is the essential epistemic route to a new realm of beings [that we think about]" (p. 5). See also Annas (1981) for a discussion of the objectifying role of mathematical definitions as traced though several Platonic dialogues.

metamathematical theory. We can now clearly see why the *part of* Platonist interpretations, of Cornford, White, Tait, and Benson, fail to hit their mark. Recall that these Platonist perspectives arise in light of the mathematicians' supposed failure to give a first-principled account of their hypotheses; having seen the supposed error of their ways, the mathematician should now be motivated to adopt the philosophers' dialectical method and so search for those unhypothetical first principles that would allow them to give an account of these in terms of a domain of stable mathematical objects (i.e., as either geometrical or philosophical forms). But, as I have shown, the mathematician can rest easy in their use of the method of hypothesis and in the metamathematical use of the geometric theory of proportion to give such a foundational account of their objects as objects of thought, *without* having to adopt the philosopher's dialectical method.

Moreover, what we require of such a metamathematical *foundation*, if I may, yet again, use this term in an *organizational* sense[59] is that it provides an overarching good-ordering account of what constitutes a good order of the "kinds of things" we think about. The geometric theory of proportion, for example, tells us that we should think about numbers *as if* they were geometrically constructed measures, or measures of ratios, but it does not tell us that numbers *are* such things – again, this would be to confuse an account of things "in accordance with belief" with those "in accordance with being." This marks the point of my disagreement with Tait (2002); he sees Plato's foundational goal as one that aims to "make explicit the rational structure we are studying and so to *define what is true* of the structure," whereas "[f]or Aristotle, the goal of foundations can only be organizational" (p. 2, n. 2; italics added). Forgoing any interpretation of Aristotle's organization view, I see Plato's aim of getting at the "rational structure," now read as its proportional structure, by *organizing* all the mathematical subjects in terms of geometric measures or ratios. As already noted, properly speaking, the geometric theory of proportion does not itself have a subject matter; borrowing Burnyeat's (2000) terminology, it provides an "abstract schema" (p. 73) for organizing the subject matters of the various disciplines, but it itself is not about anything, or in Plato's terms, it is not "in accordance with being." As a result, it cannot, as Tait suggests, "define what is true." But this is no fault. While it was certainly the case that the geometric theory of proportions was not fully developed at the time of the writing of the *Republic*, it was certainly being developed, and, as I have shown, Plato was well aware both of its geometrical developments and of its

---

[59] See Landry (2013).

arithmetical alternatives. This is yet another reason why, even at the highest level of mathematical investigation, Plato would still hold the principles of the geometric theory of proportion as hypothetical – that is, *as if* they were true.[60]

The geometrical theory of proportion, even if taken as hypothetical, provides us with a foundation as an overarching good-ordering account of the "kinds of things" of mathematics, and in so doing, it allows us to "acquire a systematic and wholly general grasp of what each thing is" by providing us with *methodological first-hypotheses* (e.g., the hypothesis that numbers are geometrical measures). But it is not a "foundation" in the current philosophy of mathematics sense of the term, that is, it does not provide *metaphysical first-principles*[61] that would allow us claim that it "defines what is true" and so presume that such things metaphysically exist. To think that it should is, simply, to confuse the method of mathematics with the method of philosophy. Tait's stronger foundational claim, and his result-ing Platonist interpretation, arise from just this confusion. He holds, in line with White (1976), that "Plato was concerned to argue for a proper founda-tion for them (the so-called *mathēmata*)" (Tait 2002, p. 1), but, "whereas White understands the new foundations to be a new and separate science of *dialectics,* with its own axioms and theorems, on [Tait's] account the foundations is to consist in adequate first principles for, say, geometry, itself, to be founded by a *process* of dialectic" (p. 2, n. 1).

Our reconsiderations, at both the mathematical and metamathematical level, clearly show that the mathematical Platonist story, by confusing the hypothetical method of mathematics with the dialectical method of philoso-phy, conflates the two types of realism at play in Plato's *Republic*: *methodo-logical* realism and *metaphysical* realism. I have shown that while Plato is

---

[60] McLarty (2005) shares this view:

> Probably these subjects developed a great deal during Plato's life (perhaps 427–347 BC) and from then until Euclid ... *Hypotheses rose and fell and led to more* – that is hypotheses not only in the sense of conjectures, but also of axioms and problems and methods and concepts chosen as true, productive, and revealing (cf. *Meno* 86–87). Could Theaetetus and Eudoxus create new theories of irrationals, proportions, and solids, without Plato knowing they conceived and tested and destroyed many hypoth-eses? ... if the histories are true then Theaetetus and Eudoxus faced and offered a good many refutations *and Plato knew it*. (p. 130; italics added)

[61] As McLarty (2005) rightly points out: "There is no talk of raising them (the reformed subjects of astronomy and harmonics) higher (than hypothesis), nor of raising geometry (to a foundation). The only higher level mentioned in any Platonic dialogue is dialectic reaching the Good as an unhypothetical first principle of everything" (p. 125). Where McLarty's intermediates interpret-ation goes wrong, however, is that he misses the foundational use of the geometrical theory of proportion as itself the highest theory, and so playing an organizational role as akin to the Good.

certainly a *philosophical Platonist* – that is, he adopts metaphysical realism for philosophical inquiry – he is a *mathematical as-ifist* – that is, he adopts *methodological realism* for mathematical inquiry. Indeed, if there is one clear message that we should get from Plato, it is that we should never confuse mathematics with metaphysics! They are distinct in method and, so, *must* be distinct in both epistemology and ontology. Thus, Plato was *not* a mathematical Platonist!

Why does any of this matter for current practitioners of philosophy of mathematics? Because it shows that we too would do well to keep the methodological requirements for mathematical knowledge distinct from the metaphysical ones of philosophical knowledge. As practitioners of philosophy of mathematics, who, like Plato, undertake answering foundational or metamathematical problems, we would do well to place more focus on the mathematician's method and so on mathematical practice than we do on mathematical metaphysics. Moreover, if we insist on a metaphysical reading of Plato's view of mathematics, then, not only do we misread Plato, but we also close the door to understanding the ways in which mathematical practice itself can offer an account of mathematical methodology, mathematical epistemology, and mathematical ontology. Thus, just as Plato was not happy with current practitioners of mathematics, because they confuse mathematical images with mathematical objects, so too am I not happy with current practitioners of philosophy of mathematics, because, by confusing the metaphysical aim of having to reason to first principles with the mathematical aim of having to reason from hypotheses, they confuse mathematical objects with metaphysical forms.

The Philosophy of Mathematics

THE DIVIDED LINE

	Visible World (509d) / Becoming (521d)		Intelligible World (509d) / Being (521d)	
FACULTY	Senses (510d) / Perception (511d)		Soul (510b) / Reason (510b)	
SUBJECT			Mathematics	Philosophy
METHODOLOGY			Hypothetical (510b) • Hypotheses as if first principles • Down from hypotheses to conclusion (510b,511a) • ~Dialectic (531d,534a) • Dreaming about what is (533b) • Dream about reality (534d)	Dialectical (511b) • Hypotheses as hypothesis • Up to unhypothetical first principles from hypotheses (510b, 511b) • Account of being (534b)
	Opaque (519d, 511e)	Clear (509d, 511e)	Opaque (509d, 511e)	Clear (511c, 511e)
EPISTEMOLOGY	Opinion (510a) **Belief** (534a)		Knowledge (510) **Understanding** (534a)	
	Imagination (511e, 534a)	Belief (511d-e) **Opinion (534a)**	Thought (511a-e, 534a) ~Knowledge (514d, 533c)	Understanding (511b-d) **Knowledge (534a)**
ONTOLOGY	Images, shadows, reflections (509e-510a)	Animals, plants, artifacts (510a)		
		• Mathematical images (510b) • Diagrams, figures (510d-e, 511a) • Images of physical objects (510b) • visible forms (510d) • images drawn (510e) • numbers attached to visible images (525d) • motions of ornaments of the heavens (529)	• Mathematical objects themselves (510e) • the odd, the even, the figures the three angles as hypotheses (510c) • square, diagonal itself (510e) • things themselves (510e) • numbers themselves (525d) • true motions measure by numbers (529d) *Geometric theory of proportion as the highest mathematical theory (531c-d, 534)	• Forms themselves (510b, 511b-c) • Good itself as the highest form (509e, 533b, 534c)

Translations:
Eikasai as Imagination
Pistis as Belief
Doxa as Opinion
Dianoia as Thought
Episteme as Knowledge
Noesis as Understanding.

Note: Bold indicates a change in terms used.

Figure 1

References

Annas, J. (1981), *An Introduction to Plato's Republic*, Oxford: Oxford University Press.

(2003), *Aristotle's Metaphysics: Books M and N*, Oxford: Oxford University Press.

Balashov, Y. (1994), "Should Plato's Line Be Divided in the Mean and Extreme Ratio," *Ancient Philosophy*, 14, 283–95.

Benson, H. H. (2003), "The Method of Hypothesis in the *Meno*," *Proceedings of the Boston Area Colloquium in Ancient Philosophy*, 18, 95–126.

(2006), "Plato's Method of Dialectic," in H. H. Benson (ed.), *A Companion to Plato*, Oxford: Blackwell, 85–89.

(2008), "Knowledge, Excellence, and Method in Republic 471c–502c," *Philosophical Inquiry*, 30, 87–114.

(2010), "Dialectic in the Republic: The Divided Line 510b–511d," in M. McPherran (ed.), *Plato's Republic: A Critical Guide*, Cambridge: Cambridge University Press, 188–208.

(2012), "The Problem Is Not Mathematics, but Mathematicians: Plato and the Mathematicians," *Philosophia Mathematica*, 20 (2), 170–99.

Broadie, S. (2020), *Mathematics in Plato's Republic*, Milwaukee: Marquette University Press.

Brumbaugh, R. (1954), *Plato's Mathematical Imagination*, Bloomington: Indiana University Press.

Burnyeat, M. F. (2000), "Plato on Why Mathematics Is Good for the Soul," *Proceedings of the British Academy*, 103, 1–81.

Cherniss, H. (1951), "Plato as Mathematician," *The Review of Metaphysics*, 4 (3), 395–425.

Cornford, F. M. (1932), "Mathematics and Dialectic in the Republic," *Mind*, 41, 37–52.

Dreher, J. P. (1990), "The Driving Ratio in Plato's Divided Line," *Ancient Philosophy*, 10, 159–72.

Foley, R. (2008), "Plato's Undivided Line: Contradiction and Method in Republic VI," *Journal of the History of Philosophy*, 46 (1), 1–24.

Fowler, D. (2003), *The Mathematics of Plato's Academy*, Oxford: Oxford University Press.

Kung, J. (1987), "Mathematics and Virtue in Plato's *Timaeus*," in J. Anton and G. Kustas (eds.), *Essays in Ancient Greek Philosophy*, Albany: State University of New York Press, 309–39.

Landry, E. (2012), "Recollection and the Mathematician's Method in Plato's *Meno*," *Philosophia Mathematica*, 20 (2), 143–69.

———(2013), "The Genetic versus the Axiomatic Method: Responding to Feferman 1977," *Review of Symbolic Logic*, 6 (1), 24–50.

McLarty, C. (2005), "'Mathematical Platonism' versus Gathering the Dead," *Philosophia Mathematica*, 13(2), 115–34.

Miller, M. (1999), "Figure, Ratio, Form: Plato's Five Mathematics Studies," *Aperion*, 32 (4), 73–88.

Panza, M. and Sereni, A. (2013), *Plato's Problem: An Introduction to Mathematical Platonism*, London: Palgrave Macmillan.

Reeve, C. D. C. (trans.) (2004), *Plato: Republic*, Indianapolis: Hackett Publishing Company.

Robins, I. (1995), "Mathematics and the Conversion of the Mind, *Republic* vii 522c1–531e3," *Ancient Philosophy*, 15, 359–91.

Robinson, R. (1953), *Plato's Earlier Dialectic*, Oxford: Oxford University Press.

Sayre, K. M. (1983), *Plato's Late Ontology: A Riddle Resolved*, Princeton University Press.

Shorey, P. (trans.) (1994), *Republic*, in E. Hamilton and H. Cairns (eds.), *Plato: Collected Dialogues*, Princeton: Princeton University Press, 575–844.

Smith, N. (2018), "Unclarity and the Intermediates in Plato's Discussions of Clarity in the *Republic*," *Plato*, 18, 97–110.

Tait, W. W. (2002), "Noesis: Plato on Exact Science," in D. B. Malament (ed.), *Reading Natural Philosophy: Essays in the History and Philosophy of Science and Mathematics*, Chicago: Open Court, 1–30.

———(2005), *The Provenance of Pure Reason: Essays in the Philosophy of Mathematics and Its History*, Oxford: Oxford University Press, 178–97.

Vlastos, G. (1988), "Elenchus and Mathematics: A Turning-Point in Plato's Philosophical Development," *The American Journal of Philology*, 109, 362–96.

White, N. (1976), *Plato on Knowledge and Reality*, Indianapolis: Hackett Publishing Company.

Whitehead, A. N. (1929), *Process and Reality: An Essay in Cosmology*, Cambridge: Cambridge University Press.

Zoller, C. (2007), "Plato on Hypothesis, Proportion, and the Education of Philosophers," *Auslegung*, 29 (1), 45–46.

Acknowledgments

This Element has been at least ten years in gestation. Thanks to all the philosophical midwives who contributed something to my goal, making it anything other than a labor in vain!

Special thanks and recognition go to Aldo Antonelli, Brad Armour-Garb, Hugh Benson, Katherine Brading, Jim Brown, Margaret Cameron, Greg Damico, Christopher Healow, Colin McLarty, Marco Panza, Stewart Shapiro, Bill Tait, Robert Thomas, and Nicholas White. Finally, I thank my friends and colleagues who have, especially in the past seven years, readily shared smiles and stories, allowing me to return to research with a renewed excitement.

With joy and love, I dedicate this Element to Kiko, Ricky, Catherine, Michael, and Paul.

Cambridge Elements ☰

The Philosophy of Mathematics

Penelope Rush
University of Tasmania

From the time Penny Rush completed her thesis in the philosophy of mathematics (2005), she has worked continuously on themes around the realism/anti-realism divide and the nature of mathematics. Her edited collection *The Metaphysics of Logic* (Cambridge University Press, 2014), and forthcoming essay "Metaphysical Optimism" (*Philosophy Supplement*), highlight a particular interest in the idea of reality itself and curiosity and respect as important philosophical methodologies.

Stewart Shapiro
The Ohio State University

Stewart Shapiro is the O'Donnell Professor of Philosophy at The Ohio State University, a Distinguished Visiting Professor at the University of Connecticut, and a Professorial Fellow at the University of Oslo. His major works include *Foundations without Foundationalism* (1991), *Philosophy of Mathematics: Structure and Ontology* (1997), *Vagueness in Context* (2006), and *Varieties of Logic* (2014). He has taught courses in logic, philosophy of mathematics, metaphysics, epistemology, philosophy of religion, Jewish philosophy, social and political philosophy, and medical ethics.

About the Series

This Cambridge Elements series provides an extensive overview of the philosophy of mathematics in its many and varied forms. Distinguished authors will provide an up-to-date summary of the results of current research in their fields and give their own take on what they believe are the most significant debates influencing research, drawing original conclusions.

Cambridge Elements ☰

The Philosophy of Mathematics